Pomona A to Z

David Allen
Inland Valley Daily Bulletin Columnist

ISBN: 978-1-938349-19-5

Library of Congress Control Number: 2013904565

The columns in this book first appeared in the Inland Valley Daily Bulletin July 18, 2004-July 3, 2005 and are used with permission of the Inland Valley Daily Bulletin. All rights are retained by the Inland Valley Daily Bulletin.

Photo credits by staff photographers: Thomas R. Cordova, Therese Tran, Walter Richard Weis, Marc Campos, Diana Mulvihill, and Will Lester. Additional photos from Cal Poly Pomona and the National Hot Rod Association. All photos used by kind courtesy of the Inland Valley Daily Bulletin.

Book Design by Mark Givens
Front Cover photo by Sally Egan
Back Cover photo by Berit Givens

First Pelekinesis Printing 2014

www.pelekinesis.com

Pomona A to Z

David Allen

*To the citizens of Pomona and to Merriam C. Webster.
Without them, this book would not have been possible.*

Foreword

Certain letters come to mind when I think of my friend and media colleague, David Allen. There is 'F' for funny. 'C' for curious. 'W' for witty. And 'KID' for kind, intelligent and determined.

David and I know each other through our ramblings: his in newspaper; mine on the radio. Our common bond is telling stories we hope will enlighten, inform, and entertain our readers and listeners. Together we occasionally try out new restaurants — places that inform his regular column — and we run into each other at an unusually high rate: Union Station in downtown Los Angeles and at the L.A. County Museum of Art, just in 2013 alone! We also sat side by side in a top-down vintage Corvette during the 2011 Pomona Christmas Parade. He received far more standing ovations than I. It must have been his fedora and tie.

Thankfully, I am a hair older than David, and a Pomona native, so my historical knowledge and personal experiences undoubtedly run deepest but, hey, he has the column, he wrote about it, so he gets the book. And what a fun book it is.

Reading it, I was reminded how strongly my affection for Pomona continues today. Sure, I miss the clock tower at the Fairgrounds, the downtown heliport, Shelton's turkey ranch, General Dynamics where my father and grandfather worked, and much more. But I also appreciate the burgeoning arts colony alongside the railroad tracks, even though my childhood Orange Belt and Kress stores are gone. The same holds true for Village Academy, the school that now sits on East Holt Avenue where Zody's once sold me cassette and 8-track tapes.

Pomona A to Z returns to the First Letter Oriented columns David wrote a decade ago. Each promotes a prominent part, or preeminent person, of Pomona's popular, peerless, and powerful past — and present. (Sorry, I couldn't get the P column out of my mind.) As I read the advance copy, I quickly moved from my easy chair to the computer so I could Google one person or place after another. Take for example the D, O, and W stories. "Really?" I asked myself. "Is this true? I had no idea! What else is there?!"

For people new to the San Gabriel Valley's easternmost big city, this book gives you a treasure chest full of history that you may yet discover in person if you take yourself on a tour. Take some appreciative friends along. Compare old images in the book to today's landscapes for a glimpse at Pomona's past. For more tenured dwellers, we who grew up in the Goddess City, many of the names and tales put us back into our childhoods. You will undoubtedly be reminded of people and places, and then fondly recall your own personal history with them.

And, if you are fortunate, you can ask a parent or grandparent who was raised here what they remember. I did that with my mother who purchased a tract house with my dad when they were married in 1956. She still resides there, just east of Lincoln Park.

Perhaps David's next quest (cue the email and letter writing campaign!) will be an A to Z guide to this region's cities: Arcadia, Baldwin Park, Claremont, Chino, Diamond Bar, Duarte ...

That'll keep him curious and determined.

As you read *Pomona A to Z*, I encourage you to come up with your own list of First Letter associations. I could not help myself — in part because I am a renowned sap, but also because I embrace our fair city's heritage, and my place in it.

My Pomona experience begins in the late 1950s. Do any of these ring a bell for you?

Alpha Beta

Buffums, Bit'O'Sweden

Crystal Cafeteria, Chicken Delight

Densmore

Emerson

First Lutheran, F&H Tire

General Dynamics, Dr. Albert Goldstein

Herb Wakeman

Indian Hill

Jenkins, Johnny Catron

KWOW

Larry Wellins Jewelers

Market Basket, Miller's Outpost

Nash's

O.H. Gehrke, Orlando's

Pack 135

Q (um...)

Reservoir

Seapy's

Troop 116

Uncle Carl Roe

Vejar

Wisconsin St.

X (aw, come on)

YMCA

Zody's, Zbinden

Happy reading!

Steve Julian
Public Radio Host, 89.3 KPCC
Los Angeles, California

Pomona and Me

Pomona, the subject of these collected newspaper columns, is a city of 160,000 at the eastern edge of Los Angeles County, and on the outskirts of the San Gabriel Valley and the Inland Empire. This all conspires to make Pomona a recognizable name but a distant locale for all but its neighbors, so near and yet so far.

For much of Southern California, the city is best known as the site of the county fair. Pomona is L.A.'s country cousin, routinely invoked with a wink in TV and movies. "They'll love it in Pomona," William Holden's writer deadpans to Gloria Swanson's washed-up film siren in "Sunset Boulevard" (1950), after hearing the lurid plot of her comeback vehicle.

In modern times, as the city's fortunes plunged, Pomona's cultural reputation has drifted toward the seedy and strange. This is encapsulated by the stoner characters in "Grandma's Boy" (2006), one of whom says of an unlikely character named Dr. Shakalu, who has promised to procure a lion for him, "I met the doctor at a cockfight in Pomona."

Locally, and less flamboyantly, people with long memories will tell you Pomona was home to the best stores and theaters, a convenient stop for celebrities on their way to Palm Springs, a major employer thanks to a defense plant and generally a lovely place.

To them, Pomona is now a tragedy, brought low by the arrival of waves of newcomers, mostly ethnic and mostly impoverished, and the departure of the defense plant, theaters and fine stores. (Currently not a single movie theater operates within city limits.) For many outsiders, gangs, poverty and homicides overshadow anything else Pomona may have to offer. For them, the city has gone from alluring to avoided, a place to pass through quickly, doors locked.

Understandably, all this has put Pomona residents into a defensive crouch, ever-alert for slights.

Pomona and I got off to a bumpy start. In my role as columnist for the Inland Valley Daily Bulletin – a newspaper born of the merger of papers in Pomona and Ontario in the late 1980s that, in yet another slight to Pomona, chose Ontario as its home base – I slowly grew to like the city once able to see past some of its surface grime. It had an urban vibe, some cool architecture, some good restaurants, an arts scene, an improvisational approach to problem-solving and a long, roller-coaster history.

A journalist is prone to identify with the underdog, which Pomona decidedly was at the turn of the 21st century. I wrote about the city from time to time. Yet a couple of columns in late 2002, meant with the best of intentions, rubbed some the wrong way.

One column on the filming of "The Cat in the Hat" on East Second Street, for which Antique Row was made over with pastel paint and oversized props into a fantasy Main Street, took the long view, positing (correctly) that a street of antique dealers was only a transitional use. My irreverent attitude left some antique dealers fuming, one complaining to my face, "Are you the one who wrote that terrible column?" Um, you mean the one in which I encouraged people to visit?

Another, about the closing days of a beloved barn-shaped pizza parlor at Holt and Towne avenues, got a nearby homeowner riled due to my quip about the "grungy" surroundings. Didn't I know Lincoln Park was the city's finest neighborhood? While that's arguably correct, the intersection in question was not technically in Lincoln Park, was home to a liquor store and a pawn shop and was practically the city's unofficial red light district.

A certain despair crept over me. I thought I was doing my best for Pomona but was making enemies everywhere I went, or so it seemed. Writing about this prickly town was like walking through a field laced with land mines.

Rather than wash my hands of Pomona, I kept at it, but with renewed sensitivity. Understanding and listening would be required to crack this nut. It was an unrequited relationship that I couldn't give up on. I liked Pomona and I really wanted Pomona to like me back.

By mid-2004, I knew the city better, the city knew me better, and an opportunity to explore Pomona in a structured way presented itself. My June 2 column began with this item:

> "Do you picture Pittsburgh as a fascinating place? I never did until a charming, funny documentary on TV a few weeks back titled 'Pittsburgh A to Z,' which came recommended by Pomona reader Peter Apanel. Why am I telling you this? Because after we compared notes on the show, Apanel asked me: 'So, when are you going to do "Pomona A to Z"?'

"Well, there's no time like the present. Let me explain how the PBS show worked first, and then I'll ask for your help. Hey, be glad this isn't a pledge drive.

"Over 90 minutes, WQED-TV documentarian Rick Sebak devoted short segments to one unusual person, place or thing in Pittsburgh for each letter of the alphabet – often not the obvious choices either. D was for a museum of daguerreotype photos, F was for fish sandwiches and U was for the veteran ushers at Pirates games, for example. Even with no particular interest in Pittsburgh, I found the show delightful. (Check shopwqed.org for more.)

"I got to wondering if I could somehow borrow Sebak's approach – because 'steal' is so negative, isn't it? – and do something similar in this space. As the most urban community we cover, Pomona has plenty of history and culture. And like Pittsburgh, its name starts with a P. What more justification do I need?

"Besides, Pomona could use some good news. Let me make one thing clear: G will not stand for gangs. We're keeping this fun and positive, OK?

"What I'm plotting is a series of

17

column items, one for each letter of the alphabet, each devoted to a quirky aspect of Pomona. I've been jotting down ideas, but some letters have me stumped, and I could use tips from people with a deeper knowledge of Pomona.

"Don't feel compelled to send 26 ideas, but your suggestions of Pomona traditions, entrenched businesses, colorful people, surprising history and unusual attractions are invited. Send 'em to me at one of the addresses at the end of today's column. I thank you, and the letter Z thanks you."

Two days later, I reported that 11 emails had already come in. Also, that I'd awakened from a dream about "Pomona A to Z" to jot down three ideas. Clearly this series had energized my conscious and subconscious both.

The result was a 26-part series over 2004-05 devoted to something unique or distinctive in Pomona for each letter, with each entry, like Sebak's, beginning with a few runnerup choices to increase the "wow" factor. Filling the space was easy enough that I wrote full columns, not the shorter items I had anticipated.

Each main selection was a person, place, or thing still in existence. I took that approach to combat people's tendency to view Pomona as a lost cause, where all the good things were gone by, say, 1965. My underlying message was: "Stop pining for the glory days! There's plenty in Pomona RIGHT NOW to be proud of!"

As you'll see in the columns ahead, I ranged across geographic and ethnic lines to present a cheery but accurate portrait of modern-day Pomona. Each week, one of my three columns – Sunday's, which had the most readership – was an entry in "A to Z." This pace proved impossible to sustain, and the series ultimately took a year to complete. When I reached Z, I was sorry, and yet relieved. A 26-part series? What was I thinking?

I had idle thoughts of writing "A to Z's" for other local cities, but the prospect proved daunting, and committing that much column space over an extended period to one idea began to seem impractical.

Still, even if the experiment has never been repeated, I remain inordinately fond, and proud, of "Pomona A to Z," the most ambitious project I've ever attempted. It always seemed like a natural for a collection like this, and when publisher Mark Givens approached me in 2012 about producing a book, "Pomona A to Z" was the concept I pitched.

David Allen

In some ways, these columns are out of date, no question. Updating them would have been a fool's errand; once headed down that road, many of the pieces would have had to be completely re-reported and rewritten, as the original sources have moved on, retired or died. This labor would have made the entries current, and yet still a product of 2004 thinking. We've opted, then, to leave them alone. Instead, introductions to each letter offer commentary, background and any factual updates of which I'm aware.

We're calling this a 10th anniversary edition – and publishing it precisely a decade after the series' July 18 debut – and with luck, that will excuse all. This is now history, and you can't rewrite history!

A "Pomona A to Z" produced in 2014 might be very different from the 2004-05 version, as would ones in 2024 or 1994. Consider mine a series of snapshots of a city that's always evolving in fascinating ways.

My own relationship with Pomona has also evolved. In 2007 I was grand marshal of the city's Christmas parade, a rare honor indeed for a journalist. I'm a thorn in the side of some – inevitable given my years of light mockery of City Council meetings – and no doubt only tolerated by those who don't like, or who misread, my columns. My role, too, is a specialized one; because my own shorthand description of what I do is "humorous journalism," I avoid most of the city's truly serious or divisive matters.

But by this point, most of the people I deal with recognize me as someone sympathetic to their city. At last I get the benefit of the doubt, an outcome that seemed out of reach as the century dawned, and that turnabout has been sweet indeed. I cherish my bond with that city.

I don't know how this book, my first, will be received. But my hope is that they'll love it in Pomona.

Marc Campos

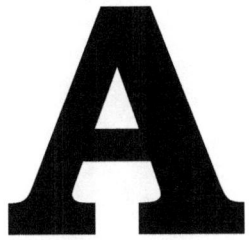

Starting my alphabetical survey with adobes – namely, the two surviving homes from the mid-1800s that are open to the public and constitute a living reminder of Pomona's origins – was the obvious way to go.

You'll note that each entry in this series opens with alliteration. Silly, intentionally so, but it was a way to get the readers' attention, provide continuity and start with a light touch.

One update to the runnerups: The Arby's on Garey Avenue closed in 2012.

This column was published July 18, 2004.

A is for Adobes

'Pomona A to Z' starts at city's beginnings

Pomona is a cool, classic, crazy city, and that's using only the letter C. I'll be employing 26 letters to describe Pomona as I highlight one neat thing about the city for each letter of the alphabet.

Call it "Pomona A to Z," a humble attempt to shine a positive light on some of the city's most fascinating corners. As mentioned previously, this is a frank ripoff of "Pittsburgh A to Z," a marvelous WQED-TV documentary by Rick Sebak. Except mine won't have the Steelers.

Let's start with Letter A candidates, of which Pomona has an awesome array:

* Antique Row and the Arts Colony — but who can choose between them?

* Agriculture, which gave Pomona its start and its name.

* The Arby's on Garey, built in the original chuckwagon style.

* Angelica Textiles, a commercial laundry dating to 1885 that's still in business.

* Richard Armour, a humorist whose memoir "Drug Store Days" is a fond reminiscence of his father's turn-of-the-century Pomona pharmacy.

An abundant assembly! But in this little survey, A will stand for Adobes.

La Casa Primera: Pomona's oldest piece of real estate, which dates back to 1837.

Luis Guerrero greeted me last Sunday outside La Casa Primera, the first home built in Pomona. It was built from adobe brick in 1837, back when California was still part of Mexico.

Guerrero, a 23-year-old docent, led me inside the one-story home on that sweltering day.

The main room was almost chilly.

"I like to keep the door closed so when you step in, you can really feel the difference in temperature. The adobe walls really keep it cool," Guerrero said.

Although the first room is set up as a parlor, it was originally a bedroom. It slept seven.

Seven? Not so different from a lot of Pomona homes today, I said, and Guerrero agreed.

"That's why when Latino families come in, they say, 'We've been there, it happens,'" Guerrero joked.

The home was built by a man named Ygnacio Palomares, a name that rolls like the Ganesha Hills.

He and his business partner, Ricardo Vejar, were given 15,000 acres of former mission land by the governor of Mexico for their cattle operation. That's essentially modern-day Pomona, Claremont, San Dimas, La Verne and Glendora.

Quite a spread. As Palomares was reputed to have told a friend, quoted in a history by Bess Adams Garner: "All these fertile leagues of land are mine. Every smoke you see rising is from the home of one of my children or one of my friends to whom I have given land."

Lord of all he surveyed, Palomares lived for 17 years in Pomona's original starter home. In 1854 he traded up to larger digs with 13 rooms.

He gave the first home to a son, Francisco – avoiding a test of Pomona's nascent real-estate market.

His second home is known as the Palomares Adobe, and it's still here too. Volunteer Gena Carpio gave me a tour of the gracious, T-shaped home.

Nice joint, although I can't say much for the family's taste in art. Three framed wreaths on the walls are woven from – ugh – human hair. (A waste of good hair, that's what I say.)

Carpio, 21, was recently involved in a "mudding party" that renovated a wall at the edge of the property. Since the wall is adobe, fixing it simply meant hurling mud at it. "Straw, water, dirt – mix it together and you get bricks that last a lifetime," Carpio told me.

Or in the case of Palomares' two adobes, several lifetimes.

TO VISIT: La Casa Primera is at 1569 N. Park Ave. at McKinley; the Palomares Adobe is at 491 E. Arrow Highway at Orange Grove. Both are owned by the city of Pomona and opened to the public by the Historical Society of the Pomona Valley. Hours are 2 to 5 p.m. each Sunday only. A $2 donation is requested.

Onward to B. I considered writing about the Barbara Greenwood Kindergarten but decided highlighting an early 20th-century building was too similar to A and its adobes. I wanted to stake out more modern territory to keep readers guessing.

Midcentury architecture has become better appreciated in the decade since I wrote this. Like Pomona, I must be ahead of my time.

To update the B nominees, the Blockbuster Concert Series went bust. Too bad.

This column was published July 25, 2004.

B is for Becket

'Pomona A to Z' builds up famed architect

Week two of "Pomona A to Z," my series highlighting the coolest parts of Pomona one letter at a time, brings us bouncing to B.

What will be B? Among the bounty:

* B could be for Barbara Greenwood Kindergarten, the nation's first standalone kindergarten, a 1908 building on the National Register of Historic Places.

* The Blockbuster Concert Series in Ganesha Park, this year scheduled for Aug. 7, 14 and 21.

* Boxing, after championship boxer "Sugar" Shane Mosley of Pomona and the respected Fist of Gold pugilism program.

* Buffums', the beloved department store downtown that's now a medical school.

* Or, for that matter, the store on Garey whose name sums up its philosophy: Buy Two, Get One Free. (Alas, the store wasn't there the last time I checked. Perhaps Buy Two gave away too many One Frees.)

But our B isn't any of those. Instead, B is for Becket's Bold Buildings.

I'm referring to Welton Becket (1902-1969), one of L.A.'s most celebrated architects.

His firm was responsible for such mid-century icons as – take a deep breath – the Dorothy Chandler Pavilion, Mark Taper Forum and Ahmanson Theater, UCLA's Medical Center and Pauley Pavilion, Bullock's department stores, the Capitol Records tower, LAPD's Parker Center, the Cinerama Dome, the Sports Arena – still with me? – Century City Shopping Center and the Pan Pacific Auditorium.

Pomona City Hall and the Council Chambers, left, are among Welton Becket's bold buildings.

And Pomona's Civic Center!

In the 1960s, Becket's firm designed seven buildings in downtown Pomona: six in the Civic Center, plus Buffum's.

It's the largest concentration of Becket's work anywhere, according to the L.A. Conservancy, which sponsored a retrospective and tour, "Built By Becket," in 2003.

Stroll around the Civic Center and you feel like you're in "The Jetsons," that other 1960s-era vision of the future.

There's the Council Chambers, a round building similar to the Taper Forum that seems to float. City Hall with its thin vertical windows and glass pavilion entrance. The Library's expansive interior without internal columns.

Other Becket buildings nearby are the Police Department, Superior Courts and Public Health Building.

With its parklike setting and broad walkways stamped with the Pomona logo, the Civic Center has a Utopian feel, like something out of the sci-fi film "Logan's Run."

"Those were buildings of the future, and that's what Pomona wanted," said Mike Schowalter, founder of the Pomona Modern Committee, which dotes on 1950s and '60s architecture.

On Wednesday, Schowalter gave me a tour and the back-story.

You see, by the late 1950s Pomona was faced with a decaying downtown as shoppers fled to the glitzy Pomona Valley Center and its Sears on the outskirts of town.

In a bold stroke, the city decided to reinvent its core with a downtown pedestrian mall and a modern Civic Center.

Six of 12 buildings went up before the effort ground to a halt. But get a load of what else Pomona had on the boards: a monorail station, downtown heliport, civic auditorium, planetarium, art museum and residential high-rises.

Whoa!

The future would be so bright, Pomonans would be wearing shades.

"They were on the cutting edge," Schowalter said fondly of the era's leaders. "You've got to admire a city for doing something so out there."

Speaking of out there, longtime residents may remember when – in a Mayberry-meets-"Blade Runner" moment – the reflecting pools were stocked with trout for fishing contests. The plaza was also the site of Easter sunrise services.

These days the Civic Center is the worse for wear, and the reflecting pools have been replaced with landscaping because the homeless population used the pools for bathing.

Still, most of the grandeur remains.

Hey, it's not Victorian architecture. But if you can appreciate 1960s style, heavy on exposed aggregate concrete, the Civic Center's got it in spades.

If restored, Schowalter asserted, Welton Becket's Civic Center would easily compare to Frank Lloyd Wright's modern buildings.

"This guy," Schowalter said, "was pretty hot stuff."

And so "A to Z" careens to the letter C and a topic bursting with Vitamin C. Pomona being the goddess of fruit, recognizing the city's citrus heritage was a must.

Cal Poly still has the largest citrus grove in the area, a welcome holdout from the valley's urbanization. Enrique Hernandez, who was featured in this entry, is no longer at the university, but as manager of a farm in Virginia he remains involved in agriculture.

The Cal Poly Farm Store, mentioned herein, remains one of Pomona's best-kept secrets despite the publicity here and elsewhere. So does the Pomona Concert Band. The wonderful Stan Selby, its founding conductor, died on Nov. 23, 2004, I'm sad to say, but the band soldiers on under the direction of Linda Taylor.

Among the runnerups, the fairgrounds' Clock Tower, in place since 1952, was removed prior to the 2005 Fair due to termite damage. Time takes its toll even on timepieces. It was not replaced.

This column was published Aug. 1, 2004.

C is for Citrus

'Pomona A to Z' finds groves aren't pulp fiction

Part 3 of "Pomona A to Z" brings us to the letter C, as we continue our countdown of the city's charms.

Making it to C, by the way, puts Pomona ahead of Katharine Hepburn, who was once famously panned by Dorothy Parker for a performance said to run "the gamut of emotions from A to B."

Trust me, Pomona's got more range than that.

Central among the city's C candidates:

* The Concert Band, which performs each Thursday night in Ganesha Park in the summertime under the direction of G. Stanton Selby, who's led the band since its first season – in (wow!) 1947.

* The Clock Tower, a landmark at the County Fair.

* The Carousel Chorus barbershop group.

* City of Churches, Pomona's old motto, reflecting the large number of congregations.

* Cinnamon doughnuts at Carl's, a West Holt Avenue fixture since 1956.

Culling this collection was certainly complex! But my C is of the vitamin variety, because C is for Citrus.

Citrus is still close at hand as Cal Poly Pomona's Enrique Hernandez, 33, stands amid the university's grove, the largest still left in the valley.

Pomona and the rest of the valley, as you surely know, once grew some of the best oranges, lemons and grapes in the world. The sight and sweet smell of those long-vanished groves remain fond memories for longtime residents.

But here in 2004, is there any citrus left? Backyard trees and a few small lots are all you'll find.

Except at Cal Poly Pomona!

True to its roots as an agricultural school, the college still has an expanse of orange and grapefruit trees in production as a learning tool.

"We've got about 20 acres of citrus," Enrique Hernandez, Cal Poly's farm supervisor, told me Friday.

That's about 2,000 trees, producing some 180 tons of oranges and grapefruit a year in 23 varieties.

Hernandez oversees this bounty – the largest citrus grove left in the valley.

"It's not as big as the ones that used to be here," Hernandez allowed. "But for being the last one, it's not bad."

A Cal Poly graduate who's now a full-time employee, Hernandez proudly showed me around the orange groves. Navels were recently harvested, but Valencias were still on the trees.

Walking amid the neat rows of bushy trees, dirt underfoot, I got a sense of what the valley must have been like a half-century ago.

Only the distant hum of Interstate 10 traffic, and the homes visible along the top of the hills, were reminders that this grove is more a part of the valley's past than its future.

A country boy from San Diego County, Hernandez, 33, grew up surrounded by citrus. He prefers open spaces, not tract homes on tiny lots.

I asked about the blight reputed to have killed or weakened most of Pomona's citrus trees. Pests are more of an issue today. That and urbanization – "creeping 2-by-4 disease," Hernandez jokingly called it.

"Pretty soon the only agriculture you'll see in Southern California is gonna be greenhouses," Hernandez said.

After I dried my tears, we visited the Farm Store at Kellogg Ranch, a campus market that has sold Cal Poly-grown produce and other select items to the public since 2001.

Fresh orange juice too, in your choice of Valencia or Mandarin.

A sign on the refrigerator case reads: "Cal Poly Pomona orange juice separates because it is pure without additives."

Right there in the store, I downed a Mandarin OJ, squeezed just hours earlier. It was so astoundingly good, it knocked my socks off.

(I found my socks later, near the

summer squash.)

The upscale, air-conditioned grocery resembles a Whole Foods or Trader Joe's except with more produce.

"We would like more people to know about it," student manager Melynda Holm said.

Let me help: Hours are 10 a.m. to 6 p.m. seven days a week, the address is 4102 S. University Drive at Temple and the phone is (909) 869-4906.

So C is for Citrus at Cal Poly. It's great to know that despite creeping 2-by-4 disease, a sliver of the valley's citrus heritage is alive and well.

Orange you glad?

Do me, a car is simply transportation, while for others, it's a religion, or a status symbol. Despite driving Toyota Corollas for two decades, I really do like the NHRA Museum at Fairplex. You can't help but be impressed by the shiny old cars on display indoors, and the obvious affection for the sport of drag racing evinced in the displays. It has that cool '50s-'60s vibe.

The National Hot Rod Association's existence is proof that when bracketed by the soothing words "National" and "Association," anything, no matter how rebellious, can be made to seem respectable. Mark my words, someday we'll see the National Eminem Association.

This column was published Aug. 8, 2004.

D is for Drags

'Pomona A to Z' gets up to speed

It's D day as "Pomona A to Z," my alphabetical survey of the city's delights, dotes on the letter D.

Which delights should we dwell on? Among the dazzlers:

* Diamond Ranch High, the hillside school whose design, by rising architect Thom Mayne, has been written up in the New York Times.

* Donahoo's, the popular take-out chicken restaurant with the fiberglass rooster on the roof.

* Dedication of Disaster City, the civil defense bunker under the Police Department whose opening in 1964 was presided over by – whoa! – nuclear physicist Edward Teller.

* Desi Arnaz, who performed at the Fox Theatre in 1947 with Lucille Ball.

What a dilemma! But after some dithering, my decision is that D is for Drags, as in Drag Racing.

Pomona didn't invent drag racing – I

think that was Ben-Hur – but the two go together like peanut butter and jelly.

The reason will rock you. Hot rodding became (gasp) respectable in large part because of the Pomona Police Department, specifically, car-loving Police Chief Ralph Parker and a young motorcycle sergeant named Bud Coons.

By 1950, hot rodders who had been racing in dry lake beds were taking it to the streets instead: peeling out, speeding, causing a racket and sometimes killing themselves or others. It was a national problem.

"In the '50s, if you were a hot rodder, it was the same as being in a gang today," Coons, now 80, told me by phone from his home in Lake Havasu City, Ariz.

One night Coons was on patrol when he saw a "real nice" Chevy, similar to one he was working on in his spare time. So he pulled over the driver for a chat.

"He thought I was going to write him up," Coons said. "I was interested in his car."

The motorist was on his way to a meeting of the Pomona Choppers car club and invited Coons, who practically caused a riot when he pulled up in uniform.

Coons explained his interest in cars, as

1962 Pomona drag races: A race official looks over a modified Corvette at the starting line.

well as his interest in safety, and found a receptive audience.

Soon he was helping to organize rally runs, shows and barbecues for racers. The Choppers were even allowed to meet in a nook of the police station. The co-opting had begun!

With a pitch from Parker, Coons and the Lions Club, the fairgrounds set aside space for a dragstrip in 1951.

Hot rodders had a controlled, legal straightaway. Deaths from speeding fell dramatically, as did complaints, Coons recalled. That prompted a writeup in an FBI bulletin to police departments nationwide about Pomona's approach.

In 1954, Wally Parks, who had just founded the National Hot Rod Association, hired a group of four hot rod enthusiasts to travel the country to promote drag racing and safety.

Among them was Coons, who took a leave of absence from the force to join what was dubbed the Drag Safari.

No, they didn't all wear dresses.

Their Dodge station wagon towed a trailer containing inspection gear and timing devices, everything they needed to run a drag race except white T-shirts and hair gel.

As a police officer, Coons commanded respect from city leaders wherever the Safari stopped. Dragstrips sprouted in their wake. Racing rules were honed.

"Pomona helped legitimize the hot rod movement and drag racing," Coons said.

Pomona also was the site of the first National Hot Rod Association-sanctioned race, in 1953, and today is home to the association's Motorsports Museum, housed in a stylish Art Deco building at Fairplex. For museum info: (909) 622-2133 or museum.nhra.com.

Amateur races still take place quarterly on the original Pomona strip, as do the professional Winternationals, to the delight of fans and consternation of neighbors.

Pomona has the oldest dragstrip in the United States still in use, and its bleachers turned drag racing into a spectator sport, museum director Sam Jackson told me.

The connection is even immortalized in song.

"GTO," the 1964 classic by Ronny and the Daytonas, has the singer expressing his desire to buy a GTO, "take it out to Pomona and let 'em know/that I'm the coolest thing around."

And that's why D is for Drags. Did you doubt it?

Coming up with a good column for the letter E wasn't, you know, easy. Not much is known about the Edison historic district, my first choice. I can't remember why I didn't write about the Ebell Club, but the club has since dissolved and its stately building deeded to the Historical Society of the Pomona Valley. The Emerger gallery, incidentally, is long gone.

For E, I went with what you might call a dark horse entry: a Cal Poly equestrian program.

Steve Wickler, the program's director and the primary source for the following entry, died May 26, 2007, at age 55. Holly Greene, then his assistant, is now director.

This column was published Aug. 15, 2004.

E is for Equine Education

A little horse sense offered in 'Pomona A to Z'

Extra! Extra! Read all about it! Letter E featured in "Pomona A to Z"!

If you came in late, each week we're examining another essential element of that endearing, eclectic entity known as Pomona, and doing so in alphabetical order.

As we eagerly embark on E, what are the possible entries?

* The Ebell Club, whose stately headquarters has been a visual tonic for passersby since 1922.

* Eldridge Cleaver, the former Black Panther who spent his final years in Pomona.

* Edison Historic District, comprising 637, 611 and the 500 block of West Second Street, all on the National Register of Historic Places.

* Espiau's, a fruit stand on Holt in the 1930s that sold "all the orange juice you can drink for a dime," and later became a popular coffee shop, now located in

David Allen

Claremont.

* Emerger, a gallery in the Arts Colony that, because people can't pronounce its name (e-mur-zhay), is familiarly known as the e gallery.

Exemplary examples, all. But our E is entirely different.

Come here often? Anakin, 7, works out under the watchful eye of Holly Greene at Cal Poly Pomona's Equine Research Center.

E is for Equine Education!

It's not that horses are getting degrees, like a bachelor of oats. But at Cal Poly

Pomona, students are learning about horses at the university's Equine Research Center, and so is the faculty.

In fact, Pomona and UC Davis have the only facilities in California devoted to the study of horses. Well, aside from the grandstand at Santa Anita.

Pomona's Equine Research Center plays with ponies more scientifically: They're put on treadmills.

"For us it provides a platform for very controlled studies," said Steve Wickler, the center's director and an animal sciences professor. "They take amazingly well to it."

To prove it, he and his assistant, Holly Greene, put a thoroughbred on the treadmill for me.

Horses, incidentally, are responsible for Cal Poly Pomona's existence.

Cornflake magnate W.K. Kellogg established a ranch for his beloved Arabian horses on what is now the Cal Poly campus. He deeded the property to the state in 1932 with the stipulation that Arabian breeding and horse shows continue – and to ensure Cal Poly's continued life, they do. Call (909) 869-2224 for details.

But back to the barn.

This day's test subject was Anakin, a 7-year-old named after the "Star Wars" character. He was a washout as a racehorse, but his gentle nature makes him a winner at Cal Poly.

Like any gym rat, Anakin was decked out in sporty fashion, colorful wraps wound around his two front legs. At least he wasn't in culottes.

A student started the treadmill and Anakin walked, transitioning into a trot as the speed increased.

"If you listen you hear two sounds," Wickler explained. Two limbs, right front and left rear, hit the treadmill diagonally, then the other two. It's an efficient gait, but not comfortable for a rider, as the horse's back rises and falls.

When the speed increased, Anakin broke into a canter, which is more of a rocking motion. Two feet were on the mat at any time. The other two touched the mat at different moments.

Then the incline feature was activated, so that Anakin was cantering at a 10 percent grade, as if running uphill.

"It increases the intensity two and a half times," Wickler said.

Feel that burn!

Exercise over, Anakin ate from a bucket of horse feed – the power bar of the equine world – and was led off to cool down. He didn't act winded, but Wickler pointed to Anakin's right rear leg. The horse's blood vessels stood out from exertion.

At the research center, veterinary and animal sciences students learn horse handling – many have never been around horses – and about horse anatomy and treatment.

Meanwhile, Wickler and Greene study how horses move and how they function at high altitude. Sometimes white markers are placed on the horse, similar to a human stress test, to calculate the amount of force on each limb.

It's a little trickier than working with people.

"With humans, you can say, 'Is this comfortable? Is this too much?' With horses, it's tough to ask them that," Wickler joked. "So we measure their metabolism."

Anakin was taking my own measure, sniffing my elbow as I took notes. It was a shame I couldn't interview him.

That way I could have learned about equine education straight from the horse's mouth.

When "Pomona A to Z" hit the letter F, people assumed I'd choose the Fox or the Fairgrounds, both logical and safe. Well, those two places are no mystery to anyone, and the long-shuttered Fox was at that point a symbol of the city's past, not its present or future. I wanted readers to think of Pomona in a fresh way.

So I picked something unexpected: French restaurants. Pomona, unusually, had two. Alas, today there are zero, as Brasserie Astuce closed in 2007, and Second Street Bistro, an Italian-French place, closed in 2011.

C'est la vie. Today, I'd probably write about the Fox, restored in 2009 to become a concert hall. But this was 2004, and that's why F was for French restaurants. Oh, and El Taco Nazo, one of the runnerups, is defunct too. Monkeys to Go, mentioned in the text, likewise packed up and left.

This column was published Aug. 22, 2004.

F is for French Food

Mon dieu! Pomona's F is for ... French Food? Oui.

Today "Pomona A to Z" flashes forward to the letter F. Which fun, fabulous facet of Pomona should be featured?

* F could focus on Fairgrounds, where the county fair last year funneled 1.3 million folks to Pomona.

* Fox Theater, a 1,700-seat Art Deco jewel built in 1931 whose 81-foot tower is a downtown landmark.

* Fish tacos at El Taco Nazo, which practically constitute their own food group for downtown clubgoers.

* Frantz Cleaners, with a nifty neon sign, drive-thru service and the motto "In By 10, Out By 4," here since 1951.

* Friar Tuck's, the valley's only bar in the shape of an English castle. It was built in 1968 as Magic Tower Burgers.

Fantastic!

But because my philosophy with this series is to avoid the obvious where possible, that scratches the Fox and the

Fairgrounds, which get plenty of ink.

So let me throw you a curve: F is for French Food!

For Pomona is home to not one, but two restaurants serving French cuisine: Brasserie Astuce and 2nd Street Bistro. Impressive, n'est-ce pas?

They're surviving despite Pomona's love of Mexican food and the usual fast-food suspects.

Not that it's easy.

"You talk to customers and they're afraid to come in because it's French," said Brasserie Astuce co-owner Leo Coulourides, a good-humored man with 25 years in food service.

His brasserie shouldn't be intimidating. It's on busy Foothill Boulevard, next door to Route 66 Classic Burgers and across the street from a Burger King.

In other words, not exactly the Champs Elysees.

"We serve the basic four food groups like everyone else," Coulourides told me. "We've got chicken, beef – it's just a few different herbs and flavors."

Speaking of different flavors, Coulourides is of Greek descent, his wife, Christina, is German and chef Miguel Mercado is Mexican. *Vive le différence!*

Their menu is regional French and the restaurant aspires to be casual, at least by French standards.

While Brasserie Astuce isn't snooty, you can order escargot, the ultimate French dish.

So, in an undercover visit, I did.

Qu'est-ce que 2nd Street Bistro? One of two French restaurants in Pomona, that's what.

An appetizer, the snails arrived on a bed of garlic mashed potatoes. My colleague Jennifer Cho Salaff, the most adventurous diner I know, was there to talk me through it.

Dark brown, curled up, escargot looked

a lot like mushrooms and had a similar taste. One or two chews of the slightly rubbery pieces and down they went.

"Are you thinking about the fact that they're snails?" Jennifer asked conspiratorially.

Until she brought it up, no. (Urp.)

Meanwhile, you can get escargot in the shell with butter at 2nd Street Bistro in the downtown Arts Colony – but I haven't.

Housed in an 1891 storefront, the bistro opened in May and quickly became a bustling lunch spot, no snail's pace about it.

Owner Alain Girard started Harvard Square Cafe and Viva Madrid, both in Claremont, and Caffé Allegro in La Verne.

Girard told me he'd always wanted to open a restaurant in downtown Pomona. That crazy dreamer.

"Pomona, it's different from Claremont," Girard admitted. "But I think there is potential here. There is definitely room for a good restaurant, which I think we've achieved here."

Girard seems as French as they come. A beefy man with a mop of shoulder-length hair, he looks like Gerard Depardieu and speaks in a strong Gallic accent.

Yet he once ran a chain of fish and chips shops in Scotland and was formerly married to an Italian. He's not running a traditional French restaurant either. Three-fourths of the menu is Italian.

"If I went totally French, I would have scared everyone," Girard confided.

French items include quiche Lorraine, goat cheese salad, mussels and French onion soup ("of course," Girard said).

Needless to say, while the Arts Colony has a Frenchier ambience than all-American Route 66, the funky, punky arts district isn't the Left Bank.

"I'm sure that can be discouraging for people to come and eat," Girard allowed, "but that's part of downtown Pomona life, you know?"

True. His bistro co-exists happily with its neighbor to the west, an edgy store named Monkeys to Go.

Hmm.

With a French neighbor, shouldn't that be Surrender Monkeys to Go?

Every now and then it's fun to write a column to appeal to the younger crowd and publicly renew my I'm-not-dead-yet credentials. It's also fun to try to explain such topics to the generally older crowd reading me.

Since this column, many other big names have played the Glass House, the club is no longer all-ages for every show, the exterior and interior have been renovated, the White Stripes returned (and later broke up), employees Eric Milhouse and Erik Palma have moved on, and co-owner Perry Tollett has opened a Glass House Record Store and a bar, named Acerogami, next door. Oh, and the Goddess Pomona was dropped from the county seal.

This column was published Aug. 29, 2004.

G is for Glass House

Top concerts a stone's-throw away

Greetings! It's a gala day here as "Pomona A to Z" gets the letter G in its greedy grasp. Which G meets my goal of showing Pomona's greatness?

Glom these gems:

* Goddess Pomona, the Roman deity of fruit, who is not only the city's icon but the dominant image in Los Angeles County's official seal.

* Ganesha Park, one of the valley's most gracious green spaces, nestled amid the picturesque Ganesha Hills.

* Garey, Gibbs and Gordon, three downtown streets named for investors who built Pomona.

* Grilled burgers at Golden Ox, the burger palace mentioned in Kem Nunn's crime thriller "Pomona Queen."

Good stuff! Yet our G, as you might guess, is another G entirely: The Glass House.

There's no sign outside and the 84 feet of windows along West Second Street reveal what looks like a vacant storefront.

Yet young people of all shapes, sizes and hair colors line up around the block to get in when the Glass House has a show.

Thrifty Drugs is long gone, but music fans still find low, low prices at the Glass House, where a live show can be cheaper than a CD.

The low-key concert venue manages to attract top-flight alternative-rock acts to good ol' Pomona.

It started with No Doubt, which opened the club with a two-night stand on Jan. 25 and 26, 1996. Among the performers since then: Sonic Youth, the White Stripes, Beck, Weezer, Tricky, the Hives, Sleater-Kinney and the Pixies.

That's right, the Pixies! Wow!

NOTE TO BAFFLED READERS: If these names mean nothing to you, don't panic. You're not old and out of touch! Are you kidding? Music was *way* better in your era ("your era" being anywhere from the 1930s to the mid-1990s). Yes, yes, it's all a bunch of noise today, ever since the jitterbug. I understand. Forget I brought it up.

So, anyway.

Many bands play one show in an L.A. club and also play a night at the Glass House, which draws "all the kids from Riverside and Orange County" who can't get to L.A., Glass House manager Eric Milhouse told me.

Brothers Perry and Paul Tollett co-founded the club to fill the void left by the demise of the Pomona Valley Auditorium and Montclair's Green Door as live music venues.

How does the 800-capacity Glass House out in the hinterlands of Pomona get such good bands?

The Tollett brothers are successful concert promoters in L.A. and they also stage the popular Coachella Music Festival in Indio, so they have connections. Also, bands often become big only after the Glass House gets them.

"Usually we get bands on the cusp of

becoming successful," said Glass House employee Erik Palma, who handles contracts.

Then again, Sonic Youth, a veteran band of more than two decades that came to Pomona in July, "wanted to play (here). They knew about the Glass House," Milhouse said.

Longtime residents will remember the building as a Thrifty Drugs, which operated from 1949 to the 1970s. Some remember the old layout.

"Where the mosh pit is, that's where they sold hair care products," building owner Ed Tessier told me. "Where the stage is now, that's where they dispensed drugs."

Rock and roll!!

Seriously, if you can look past the tattoos and piercings, the Glass House is a pretty safe environment. Unlike many clubs, all ages are allowed because no alcohol is served. Security guards are watchful.

"Our average age is 14, 15," Milhouse said. Parents can come in for free to inspect the place.

"It's kind of a neat thing to do all-ages shows. It's such a good outlet for kids," said Milhouse, 28, an earnest, soft-spoken music fan who grew up in Riverside.

"There's not a lot to do in the Inland

Empire except go to the mall," he added, "and we all know how boring that is."

On the downside, the club has virtually no seating, so aging fans like me have to figure out how to stand for three hours. (This will become easier in a few years, when I can lean on my walker.)

But what the Glass House lacks in comfort, it makes up for in value.

Tickets average $12, parking is free and Cokes are $2. I saw up-and-comers the Shins, whose music is featured in the movie "Garden State," for $19. Try getting that deal at Staples.

One memorable recent show was an April date by the Pixies. Set to play Coachella, the newly reunited band did a surprise show in Pomona the night before.

"You saw Jack Black and Zach de la Rocha singing along to every word, as into it as the kids," Palma said.

To attend the 2002 MTV Music Awards in L.A. and their Glass House show later that night, the White Stripes had to be creative.

"They flew into Pomona on a helicopter," Milhouse said. "They landed a few blocks from here."

Here's the letter H, with another choice to cater to the younger set and surprise the older set. I tried to focus on all of Pomona's ethnicities in "A to Z" at one point or another and writing about hookahs was an example.

By the way, I won a bet with an editor over this column. He wagered me lunch that I would get complaints for writing about hookahs. I said I wouldn't, and I was right. Ha ha. Hookahs have become more mainstream since this column appeared. You can now smoke hookahs in Upland, for pete's sake. And Claremont.

This column was published Sept. 5, 2004.

H is for Hookah

Pomona's H is for Hookah, and that's not blowing smoke

Hail, heroes! "Pomona A to Z" has hit the letter H, and I've hunted high and low for an H to highlight. Which H-bomb should we drop?

* H could be for horse racing, an L.A. County Fair tradition since 1933. Pomona's races that debut year are said to have been the first in Southern California to allow betting.

* Hospitality, as in the top-ranked Collins School of Hospitality Management at Cal Poly Pomona, endowed by a former owner of the Sizzler chain.

* Historical Society of the Pomona Valley and Pomona Heritage, two volunteer groups preserving Pomona's older buildings and neighborhoods.

* Hoa Binh, a popular market serving Pomona's large Vietnamese community.

* Heliport, which downtown Pomona had in the late 1960s, offering travel by helicopter.

Our H, however, is a hallmark of today's

David Allen

diverse Pomona.

Because H is for Hookah.

No, not the ones on Holt – watch the spelling! I'm talking about hookahs, as in the Middle Eastern water pipe.

In Pomona, Aladdin Jr. on Garey Avenue has a small hookah patio, as well as a top-notch buffet. A few other patios exist in other local cities. But the valley's largest and best-equipped hookah lounge is at Pomona's Sahara Cafe.

It's not the likeliest of locations. Ensconced in a shopping plaza in the Phillips Ranch neighborhood, Sahara Cafe is in the heart of suburbia – seemingly a cultural Sahara.

The cafe's outdoor patio seats 200 and is bigger than the indoor dining area. Owner Usmaan Ahmad admits that food is secondary, calling his business a hookah lounge first and restaurant second.

On a hopping night, the place is packed, with smoke

Puff piece: Ali Malik, 26, of La Verne is hookah'd on a feeling on a recent night at Pomona's Sahara Cafe.

Thomas R. Cordova

and conversation floating free and Middle Eastern pop music videos flashing on plasma TV screens.

And you thought Pomona was just enchiladas and norteno music.

So what is a hookah? It's a water-filtered pipe that has its origins in India but was perfected in Turkey some 400 years ago.

The cafe's hookahs stand about three feet tall. Tobacco is heated in a bulb at the top. Smoke is drawn through cool water at its base via a long tube that ends with a mouthpiece.

Only flavored tobaccos are offered, 11 fruit flavors in all. (It's like Snapple for the lungs.) The tobacco is a mix of ground fruit pulp, tobacco, molasses and honey "for that sweet taste," Ahmad said, adding that there's no nicotine and only a trace of tar.

"There are people who speculate how many hookahs you'd have to smoke to equal one cigarette," Ahmad said.

Sahara designates several hookahs for each flavor of tobacco to avoid any mixing. Thus, the cafe has about 150 hookahs.

I chose apple tobacco, and employee Matais Lopez hooked me up for the first smoke of anything in my sheltered life. A transplanted Midwesterner with a Middle Eastern hookah? Oh, if my hometown of

Olney, Ill., could see me now.

"You smoke it like a cigar," Ahmad instructed me. "You're not supposed to inhale."

Paging Bill Clinton!

I took a few puffs as the conversation continued. The smoke was all right – I was pleased I didn't collapse in a spasm of coughing, which might have put a crimp on the interview – but it wasn't my thing. I prefer my apple in pie form.

Ahmad said the hookah trend is skyrocketing, especially among young people, and he's proof. Just 24 today, he began smoking hookahs at lounges in Westwood while studying for his marketing degree.

Oddly enough, he was attending CSU San Bernardino, not UCLA. To drive that far he must have been hooked on hookahs.

He and his brother, Shahab, 20, bought the lounge in May when the original owner returned to Lebanon.

Their clientele is about half Middle Eastern, with the non-Middle Eastern segment growing.

For those smokers, "it's the allure of smoking something in public that's not a cigarette," Ahmad explained.

"For us, it's more cultural," continued

Ahmad, whose family is from Pakistan. "In the Middle East, they don't have bars, they have hookah lounges. You have tea and smoke 'til the early morning."

Mortgage brokers from Orange County were at a nearby table that Friday evening. They come to the lounge three or four times a week.

"For us it's like happy hour," said Issa Dugom, a Jordanian immigrant. "After work we come in, kick back, relax."

Forget Miller Beer. In Pomona, it's hookah time.

I

This one was not only fun, it was delicious. Dr. Bob's, a premium ice cream business, has been written up all over – and featured on NBC's "Today" show in 2013 – and it's based in good ol' Pomona.

Its Upland store has closed, but Dr. Bob's is sold at the county fair each fall and at its fairgrounds plant year-round (phone [909] 865-1956 for hours), at the Cal Poly Farm Store in Pomona, Wolfe's Market and I Like Pie in Claremont, and at finer restaurants.

The $3.50 price is outdated. Whatever the current price is, it's worth it. Also, one of the runnerups, the Indian Hill Cinemas, closed in 2005, leaving Pomona without a single movie theater.

This column was published Sept. 12, 2004.

1

I is for Ice Cream

You'll scream, because Pomona's I is for ice cream

My series "Pomona A to Z" continues to inch along. With the letter H last week, I imagine it's time for I, isn't it?

It is. Now, call me an idealist if you must, but Pomona's interest should be illustrated. So consult this idiosyncratic itinerary of I candidates:

* I could be for Indian Hill Cinemas, the valley's only independently owned theater. The $4 matinees revive memories of decades past, and the 1970s decor doesn't hurt either.

* Indoor Swap Meet, the place to go for inexpensive items.

* Islamic education, specifically, the City of Knowledge School, a K-12 academy that earlier this year produced a student with a 1600 SAT score.

* Indians who once roamed the Ganesha Hills.

* Indian Hill Boulevard, the most ethnic, intriguing stretch of which stops at the Claremont border.

Impressive! But before you get impatient, let me identify my choice: I is for ice cream. Namely, the plant on the Pomona fairgrounds where an exclusive brand of ice cream is made.

From cows to cone: Bob Small produces Dr. Bob's ice creams in a plant at the LA County fairgrounds.

There, Bob Small cranks out Dr. Bob's HandCrafted IceCreams, a premium label sold at upscale markets and restaurants throughout California, besides delighting fairgoers.

At $3.50 for a single-scoop cone, Small's ice cream won't be mistaken for a supermarket brand.

"We're at the high end," Small told me

with pride. "We're always the highest priced at the retail market."

Small, incidentally, isn't a medical doctor – he has a doctorate in business – but he's got the cure for what ails you, and you don't even need a prescription.

A professor who teaches wine, beer and spirits courses in Cal Poly Pomona's hospitality school, Small started Dr. Bob's in 1999 with friend Bill Baldwin as "kind of a lark."

Small develops the recipes, using premium ingredients like Scharffen Berger chocolates and real vanilla for flavors that are less sweet but more intense than most ice creams.

Among his flavors: Peach, Fig, Black Raspberry, Vanilla Peanut Butter Chunk and Brown Sugar Pecan. Dr. Bob's is defined by its chocolates, including The Works: dark chocolate ice cream spiked with three types of chips.

The top seller is still vanilla.

Dr. Bob's is a minimum 16 percent butterfat – another reason four out of five doctors don't recommend it – and is dense, too. It's about 35 percent air, compared to a startling 50 percent in most major brands.

"The less air, the more ice cream there is, and the more dense and rich the product will taste," Small said.

Dreams of a retail empire stopped at a single store in downtown Upland, but Small's wholesale business is booming. In 2003 he sold the equivalent of 30,000 gallons.

Dr. Bob's – see drbobsicecream.com – is sold in Gelson's supermarkets and scooped locally in the Sycamore Inn, Walter's, Spaggi's, The Press, Pizza N' Such and the Restaurant at Kellogg Ranch. You can buy it by the pint at Wolfe's Market and Cal Poly's Farm Store.

It's been featured on the Food Channel and just last month in *Sunset* and *Bon Appetit* magazines. Darn, I got scooped.

The Pomona plant opened in 2002 at the fair's invitation. Located across from the livestock barn, the plant does retail sales during fairtime – now through Sept. 26 – and last fair served more than 15,000 customers.

So how does Dr. Bob's crew make ice cream? Small let me behind the scenes to watch the production of two tubs of a popular flavor: Strawberry, Sour Cream and Brown Sugar.

A local dairy combines the cream and sugar to his specifications. At the plant, ice cream maker Jorge Morales put it in a 20-quart freezer for 10 minutes to thicken along with sour cream.

What came out was smooth and silky, if only partly finished. After a taste, I told Small he could do well marketing that.

"Yeah, we could," he agreed. "A sour cream ice cream. It could go with certain desserts."

Morales turned the spigot and half-filled two 2.5-gallon tubs with the mixture. He spooned in strawberry compote and cupfuls of brown sugar, stirred with a spatula, topped off the tubs with more mix, compote and brown sugar and stirred again.

Somehow I can't see Ben or Jerry doing it this way.

Smoothing the surface, Morales covered the tubs and put them in a minus-40 freezer to harden overnight.

The ice cream comes out so hard, "it's like a deadly weapon," Small joked. It's then tempered in a minus-20 freezer, the temperature at which it's sold.

I didn't have 24 hours to wait, so Small uncapped a Cappuccino Crunch, The Works and Brown Sugar Pecan for samples.

Just what the doctor ordered.

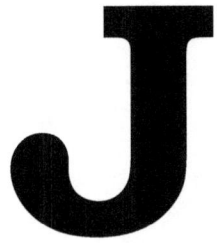

Pomona has plenty of outstanding Mexican restaurants. One local favorite is Juanita's, where you can always find people lined up on the sidewalk. Interviewing the owner proved impossible despite several attempts, as she was running not only the restaurant but a Juanita's booth at the fair, but I got enough of the story, and customers gave the piece its flavor.

The downtown jazz concerts mentioned toward the beginning are now history, and Juanita's II in Ontario, noted toward the end, became Juanita's III after a family dispute. Yes, there is no longer a Juanita's II, just as the Traveling Wilburys' records went directly from Vol. 1 to Vol. 3. Oh, and the wacky Juanita's menu board was recently simplified, the restaurant currently has an A grade and they no longer have a booth at the Fair.

The stand continues to thrive, as burrito addicts ignore the Green Burrito later incorporated into the adjacent Carl's Jr. Anyone who eats there with the real stuff next door must be nuts.

This column was published Sept. 19, 2004.

J is for Juanita's

Not to spill the refried beans, but J is for Juanita's

"Pomona A to Z," my alphabetical look at the city's jewels, now jumps to the letter J. Forgive me for jabbering, but Pomona is so jam-packed with J candidates, it's like a jamboree.

Among them:

* Jelly Donut, named the region's No. 1 doughnut shop by *Inland Empire* Magazine and a Pomona favorite.

* Jazz concerts downtown the fourth Saturday of each month.

* St. Joseph's Catholic Church, built in the Spanish Colonial Revival style and one of Pomona's largest and loveliest buildings.

* Hilltop Jamaican market and restaurant, mon.

* Jon Provost, a Kingsley Elementary student who played Timmy on TV's "Lassie" from 1957 to 1964. "What's that, Lassie? Somebody's trapped in the old well again?"

Quite a jackpot. But our jury-rigged J is none of the above, as you no doubt expected. (You're so jaded.)

Our J is Juanita's.

The waiting is the hardest part, as Tom Petty once said, and that's true at Juanita's, one of Pomona's most popular lunch spots.

A taco stand on Indian Hill Boulevard, Juanita's Drive-In has provided cheap, tasty eats for a quarter-century.

Customers swear by the place.

"The food's phenomenal with a capital F," said Steve Hammitt, 54, an insurance agent from Claremont waiting for his pork burrito last week.

Tucked between a Carl's Jr. and a 7-Eleven, Juanita's doesn't look like much. The small building with no indoor seating began as a Tastee Freez around 1956.

The food is takeout only, with two

outdoor tables for dining. You place your order at the window, pay, get a slip with your number and wait. Service is speedy, but there's almost always a few people fanned out on the sidewalk.

Naturally, Juanita's has its quirks. Like a student trying to pad a book report, the menu details every conceivable variation on its burritos and tacos, sending the combinations sprawling across three menu boards.

Say you want a pork burrito. Here are the head-spinning possibilities:

* Meat bean rice cheese $3.25

* Meat $3.25

* Meat bean cheese $3

* Meat bean rice $3

* Meat rice cheese $3

* Meat bean $3

* Meat rice $3

Can we get an organizational coach in on this? (And yes, somebody forgot "meat cheese.")

Eccentricities of the menu aside, the food is top-notch. Several diners raved about the pork. I go for the chicken-and-rice burrito myself. Some of my newsroom colleagues like the chile relleno burrito, in which a chile relleno is tucked inside a tortilla.

Juanita's is one of the great social levelers. At lunch last Tuesday, I saw all walks of humanity, from twentysomethings to senior citizens, the well-to-do to those with no visible means of support, drivers of SUVs to delivery trucks, all lined up for a five-buck lunch.

Car dealer Hal Assael, a 52-year-old who pulled up in a BMW, traveled 15 miles from Glendora, no doubt passing hundreds of other Mexican restaurants along the way, just for a chicken-and-rice burrito.

"It's the best food in town," Assael said. "I've been coming here almost 20 years."

Finn Englyng, a 27-year-old cabinet maker from Claremont, was there with three buddies.

"I think it's absolutely spectacular," said Englyng, who was waiting on an order of tacos. "I like hole in the wall places. You come to a place like this, you know you're going to get real Mexican food, not some Taco Bell or Del Taco crap."

Well said.

Of course, there is the matter of the B grade from the Health Department. As one diner told me: "I don't care about the B. If it got to a C, I'd be concerned."

Juanita's took over the spot about 1976.

The first owner, Maria Tucker, had the restaurant only briefly and, in a poignant touch, named it after an adopted daughter who died at age 5.

Tucker sold the business in 1977 to her niece, Theresa Cerna, who expanded the menu and has owned the restaurant ever since.

It's a family operation. Cerna and her husband, Jess, are often found there, as is her daughter, Marina. (A son, Ray, manages a second outlet in Ontario, Juanita's II, owned by Cerna's ex-husband.)

Theresa Cerna has had a Juanita's stand at the county fair since 2002, so she's pulling double duty right now.

Carne asada and the green chile pork are the best sellers, she told me. Tortillas are made on-site, as is the hot sauce, which comes in lidded plastic cups the size of lip balm.

Juanita's has lasted longer than any other business in that location, including the Tastee Freez, Jess Cerna told me.

"The couple that used to have the Tastee Freez," he said, "even they come here."

Nothing to explain in this one, and the only minor changes are that Katherine Staab is now the library director and, among the runnerups, that Robbins Antique Mart is now Pomona Antique Mart.

If you want the proper atmosphere for this Kellogg-themed piece, eat a bowl of cereal while reading – but don't spill milk on this book.

This column was published Sept. 26, 2004.

K is for Kellogg

Pomona's K is for a man who was truly grrreat!

Welcome back to "Pomona A to Z," where we host a kaffeeklatsch about the city's key keepsakes, bringing knowledge, and kindling respect, in those who knock Pomona in kneejerk fashion. (The knaves.)

Did you guess we're up to the letter K?

Kidding aside, Pomona has a lot of keepers among its K candidates. Among them:

* Kaiser Bill's Military Emporium, the Antique Row business whose owner, Dave George, identified the obscure military medal worn by Michael Jackson at his arraignment in January – a Serbian "bravery" medal – and was quoted worldwide.

* Kress Building, once a department store and now Robbins Antique Mart, said to be Southern California's oldest and largest such store.

* Koosh Ball, a squishy, spiky plastic gel ball created by two Pomona High alumni that was the top-selling Christmas toy of 1988.

* Walter and Cordelia (Honaday) Knott, two more Pomona High alumni, who married and founded Knott's Berry Farm.

Keen, eh? What a kaleidoscope!

Our K, however, is special. You might even say it's a Special K, because K is for Kellogg.

The man behind Kellogg's cornflakes was W.K. (Will Keith) Kellogg (1860-1951). The son of a broom maker, Kellogg never got past sixth grade, but he built a cereal empire in Battle Creek, Mich.

The cornflake king spent winters in balmy Pomona, where he established a horse ranch. He later donated the land for what became Cal Poly Pomona – the only hall of higher learning that doesn't get soggy in milk.

To learn about all things Kellogg, I met with Melissa Paul, curator of Cal Poly's W.K. Kellogg Arabian Horse Library. For the proper tone, we chatted over a breakfast of Kellogg's cereal – she had Rice Krispies, I had Frosted Flakes – in Kellogg West, a university dining hall.

After a stint as a traveling broom salesman, Kellogg went to work for his brother, nutritional pioneer Dr. John Harvey Kellogg, at his hospital and health spa.

A painting of Will Keith Kellogg (1860-1951)

The brothers experimented with cereal grains to create healthy foods for patients. Through a wacky accident in the kitchen, they came up with flakes that eventually revolutionized the way America eats breakfast.

Don't you hate it when that happens?

Although he was competitive, astute and rich, Kellogg was a shy man who treated employees well and gave away most of his wealth to help children and animals.

He especially loved horses. He had a horse as a boy that was part Arabian. His father sold it.

"It broke his heart," Paul said. "He vowed that if he ever was rich, he would buy a whole herd of Arabian horses."

Making good on his pledge, Kellogg bought 11 Arabian horses from a man in Indio in 1925, then plunked down $250,000 for 377 acres in Pomona for a horse ranch.

Lore has it a coin flip is what led Kellogg to buy the Pomona site over property in Santa Barbara.

Stables were built first so his Arabian horses would have a place to live, while Kellogg was content to rent a home in Pomona's Lincoln Park neighborhood.

Kellogg bought the best horses, many from England, and hired architect Myron Hunt to design some ranch buildings.

The ranch got plenty of visitors. They included movie stars Mary Pickford, Clara Bow, Gary Cooper, Olivia de Havilland and Tom Mix. Weekly horse shows catered to the common folk.

"Kellogg Ranch was the leading tourist

attraction in Southern California in those days," Paul said.

Kellogg Arabians were used in movies, too. One was even the model for Prince Charming's horse in Disney's "Snow White."

In 1932, Kellogg donated his 750 acres and 87 Arabian horses to the University of California. But things didn't go as planned and the property fell into disrepair.

After a public outcry, the holdings were transferred back to Kellogg and then to California State University in 1949.

Stipulations were made to ensure the horses and horse shows remained, and they do.

The first classes were held in Pomona in 1956. A decade later the campus became a full-fledged state college, bursting with snap, crackle and pop.

Kellogg died in 1951 at age 91. Though the millionaire was a modest, self-effacing fellow – "He was certainly no Donald Trump," Paul said – he's hardly a forgotten man.

Not only is his signature on every box of Kellogg's cereal, but he left his mark on Pomona by enabling the city to get the valley's only state university.

Raise a cereal spoon in his memory.

To represent the letter L, I gave serious consideration to writing about lowrider cars, knowing that's part of modern-day Pomona culture. But frankly, I had no idea where to get started on that topic. Lawn bowling was another possibility.

Instead I opted for the topic likeliest to get a "wow" from the average reader: the Laura Ingalls Wilder collection at the Pomona Public Library.

Marguerite Raybould and Lois Robbins have retired, but the library and the Wilder collection aren't going anywhere.

Call me a softie if you must, but the last quote, from Wilder's letter, makes me mist up each time I read it.

This column was published Oct. 3, 2004.

L is for 'Little House'

'Little House' fans find a home in Pomona Library

"Pomona A to Z" continues to place the city's unlimited layers in the limelight and, I hope, add luster to a sometimes hard-luck city. Now in Part 12, clearly this series is no lark.

Just as clearly, we're up to the letter L. Among the candidates worth a look:

* Lowriders, an important part of car culture in Pomona, where the movement's bible, *Lowrider* Magazine, was founded (even though the magazine later cruised down to Fullerton).

* Lawn bowling, a game popular in the United Kingdom and worldwide, still played at the Pomona Lawn Bowling Club.

* Lamp lab at Pomona's BAE Systems, a manufacturer whose lamps allow military aircraft to jam heat-seeking missiles.

* Lincoln Park, a neighborhood on the National Register of Historic Places and

one of the city's prestige addresses.

A laudatory list! Yet our lantern of learning will light upon a different L: the Pomona Library's "Little House on the Prairie" collection.

Little lasses, and even lads, have long loved the books by Laura Ingalls Wilder (1867-1957) about her childhood in the 19th century as a Western pioneer.

Little photos held by Marguerite Raybould show "Little House on the Prairie" author Laura Ingalls Wilder and her husband.

I may not be as wise as Pa, but I do know that Wilder had a special connection with the Pomona Library – an institution that isn't on the Chisholm Trail.

No, she formed that tie late in life when she corresponded with a librarian, wrote a letter to the children of Pomona, donated an autographed set of her books and even gave the library a rare gift: the original, handwritten manuscript for "Little Town on the Prairie."

And speaking of pioneers, you might say Pomona was a pioneer itself in recognizing the importance of her series.

The Pomona Library was the nation's second to honor her, naming its children's department the Laura Ingalls Wilder Room in 1950.

Wilder didn't attend – she was in her 80s, and her husband had just died – but from her home in Missouri, she wrote a letter to be read aloud. A copy is still on display.

"It makes me very proud that you have named this room in your library for me," Wilder wrote in a neat cursive. "...You make good use of your library I am sure. How I would have loved it when I was young, but I was far from a library in those days."

Far from running water and flush toilets too. From 1869 to 1879, young Laura Ingalls and her family – Ma and Pa Ingalls and sisters Mary, Carrie and Grace – lived in frontier settlements in Minnesota, Kansas, Iowa and South Dakota.

The family endured many hardships: terrible winters, poor crops, Mary's blindness and Michael Landon's curly perm.

Laura married Almanzo Wilder in 1885 and only turned author in 1932 with "Little House in the Big Woods." An immediate hit, the memoir spawned seven sequels.

One fan was Clara Webber, the Pomona children's librarian from 1948 to 1970. She corresponded with the author and hunted down Ingalls family homesites on her vacations. Even Wilder wasn't sure where they were.

"Miss Webber was really one of the first people to realize what a national treasure these books were," said Marguerite Raybould, the library's supervisor of youth services.

An alcove dedicated to Wilder displays family photos, foreign editions – such as the Swedish "Lilla huset på prärien" – character dolls and the "Little Town" manuscript in pencil.

Raybould admitted the alcove isn't exactly spellbinding stuff. What gets young readers excited is the library's annual Laura Ingalls Wilder Gingerbread Sociable, a birthday party that began in 1967, the centennial of her birth.

The party features gingerbread, an Ingalls family favorite, and period music of the type Pa played on his fiddle. About

300 children and adults attended the one in 2004.

The 2005 sociable, the 38th annual, is set for Feb. 5.

Despite changing times and demographics, children still ask for the series by name – "although it's no Harry Potter," admitted librarian Lois Robbins.

"The fact that it's a story of immigration and going to a new place with possibilities," Raybould said, "has resonance for lots of people."

So do the emotions. That's what Wilder, in her letter to Pomona's children, suggested would keep her books contemporary.

"As you read my stories of long ago I hope you will remember that the things truly worth while and that will give you happiness are the same now as they were then," she wrote.

"Courage and kindness, loyalty, truth and helpfulness are always the same and always needed."

To pay tribute to Pomona's Arts Colony, M was for Magu, the city's most lauded artist.

A couple of years after this piece, Magu moved to Ontario, and he died July 24, 2011 in La Puente. He's still an important figure in Arts Colony lore, and a memorial exhibit of his work in 2011 packed a Pomona gallery with old friends.

Among the runnerups, Mission Family Restaurant closed in December 2013.

This column was published Oct. 10, 2004.

M

M is for Magu

An up-close look at Magu, artist of note — and cars

The magnificent madness that is "Pomona A to Z," my series examining the municipality one letter at a time, this week moves to the letter M.

Which M will represent Pomona in this miscellany? Among the multitude:

* Mission Family Restaurant, a coffee shop dating to the 1940s as Hull House that still ladles up hearty fare.

* Masonic Temple, a grand building at Thomas and Fourth erected in 1909.

* Mountain Meadows Golf Course, a public course adding 18 holes of gentility to Ganesha Hills.

* Mother Smith, who in 1936 founded Casa Colina Centers for Rehabilitation.

* M & I Surplus, your one-stop shop to prepare for the apocalypse.

Marvelous! So which M will be Pomona's milestone? Showing my moxie, it's none of the above.

M is for Magu.

Who's Magu, you ask? That's Gilbert "Magu" Lujan, the pioneering Chicano artist from East L.A. who now calls Pomona's Arts Colony home.

His credo is hard to argue with.

"I aim to reflect Latino experience in art," Magu told me.

But how he does it doesn't conform to the fine arts world.

Lowrider cars, pyramids, Mexican altars and bright, bright colors are among his hallmarks.

He once put on a slide show for art students at UC Irvine. Subject: graffiti. He views it as ethnic calligraphy.

"That's not art. That's what you people do," one student told him.

Yet Magu is no primitive: He has a master's in fine arts.

As he tells it, teachers always advised him to draw from experience. Is it his fault his experience involves classic cars and junk-art barrio gardens?

Early criticism only emboldened him.

"At that point," Magu told me, "I knew I was onto something."

For three decades Magu, 64, has had fame, or at least notoriety, as a painter,

Artist Gilbert "Magu" Lujan cracks up, while a painting in progress looks on impassively.

sculptor and muralist.

In 1974, as a member of the art collective Los Four, Magu helped curate a groundbreaking exhibit of Chicano art at the staid L.A. County Museum of Art.

More recently, he designed the Hollywood and Vine subway station with car-themed art on its tiles.

Two of his pieces just left the L.A. County Fair, and more Magu is now at Pomona's dA Center for the Arts.

But let's back up. Why the nickname?

It came in adolescence when friends noticed him crowding close to art to get a closer squint, just like Mr. Magoo, the nearsighted cartoon character.

He didn't like the name but eventually

embraced it. His live/work studio is even dubbed Magulandia. His kingdom includes two subjects: his grown son, Naiche, and a friend, Ricardo Silva, both fellow artists who room with him.

Crowded with art, furniture, an upright piano and even Magu's 1954 Chevy pickup, the ground-floor studio is a former machine shop with a rollup door.

(I suppose lugging the Chevy into an upstairs loft would have been impractical.)

Encouraged by a friend, Magu moved to the nascent Arts Colony in 1999 and instantly added cachet. His new address has practical benefits over L.A.

"People ask why I live in Pomona. I say: 'Parking,'" Magu joked.

Since 1994, the colony has succeeded in populating the near-empty blocks of downtown west of Garey Avenue, and even lured a Starbucks. Yet rising property values are putting the squeeze on artists.

Magu, who said he's never made much money, cut his 3,000-square-foot space in half to economize.

Although he complains a lot, Magu's work and themes are sunnier – at least on the surface – and in conversation he frequently pauses to smile and josh.

"I'm going to tell you my secrets,"

Magu said. "Humor. I think humor softens people's view of my culture."

Whimsy and Mexican folk art traditions cloak his ideas to make them more palatable, he said.

Because Chicanos, his preferred term, are torn between two cultures and are never entirely accepted by either, they make up a third, hybrid culture, he argues.

Thus, his art employs images Latinos in the Southwest grew up on: cartoons, TV icons, altars, exaggerated cars, garish colors, cactuses, burritos and tacos.

Visual puns abound. Verbal puns pepper his conversation.

"I use the car," Magu said, "as a cultural vehicle."

I trust he wasn't steering me wrong.

a mid-alphabet break

Peter Apanel, who helped suggest this series, figured I'd do all 26 "Pomona A to Z" columns in a row, three times per week, wrapping the whole thing up in nine weeks. Yeah, they'd have loved that in Upland. Besides the need to appeal to the rest of my readership, there was also the matter of time. "A to Z" pieces took twice as long as my regular columns to research and write. Even writing one per week was proving difficult, and it was impossible to get ahead on them. So, to give myself a breather, I put the series on hiatus a few weeks.

First, though, I put out a call for reader response. J, K, L and M had passed without a single comment. Did anyone care I was doing this?

I also used the following column to explain my rationale for the series: to shine a light on Pomona but also to try to shake people out of this "glory days" mentality. Time to get over it, folks. My feeling was, let's live in the present and appreciate Pomona for what it's got now.

This column was published Oct. 17, 2004.

Pomona needs a boost

so 'A to Z' lends a helping hand

For those who came in late, it's B for Break here for "Pomona A to Z."

Yes, my series is taking a mid-point hiatus for battery recharging. Have no fear: "A to Z" will resume soon with the letter N – in November, naturally.

Consider today's column a "DVD extra," providing exclusive commentary on the series. (As with any DVD bonus, feel free to ignore it.)

Let's start with a question from reader Phyllis Willis: "Enjoying the series, and just how did you happen to choose this subject?"

Phyllis, it was a PBS documentary, "Pittsburgh A to Z," that inspired this little series of columns. As for why Pomona, I'm convinced it's the most fascinating, diverse, urban and downright funky city in the valley.

There's a second reason. Reputation-wise, Pomona is sort of the local version of Pittsburgh. It's the underdog, the gritty place everyone jokes about, puts down or avoids.

Now, Pomona's certainly got its problems, but as they say, perception lags behind reality. Unfortunately, the city's steady turnaround hasn't sunk in for a lot of people who remember only too well the bad old days when Pomona hit bottom.

Poignantly enough, those blinders are worn by a lot of Pomonans, too.

Maybe I'm stepping out on a limb here, but let me share an observation. Longtime Pomonans often rhapsodize about how great their city was in the old days and how awful it is today.

Yes, Pomona fell far and hard. But 40 years is long enough to cry over spilled milk. Besides, lost aerospace jobs and a withered downtown are hardly issues particular to Pomona.

So part of my mission with "Pomona A to Z" is to say, hey, let's appreciate Pomona for what it is, not just for what it was.

To that end, you may have noticed that every single one of my choices is still around today.

That's deliberate. Ditto with focusing some weeks on very modern aspects of Pomona, whether it's the mix of cultures or the clubs and restaurants favored by a new generation.

Enough from me. Here's what you had to say:

* Ray Bragg: "I appreciate and read with enthusiasm your 'A to Z' choices for Pomona. It is refreshing because you haven't just fallen back on the easy, 'old,' historical alphabetical choices. Instead, you have blended them with 'new' choices, because that is what makes a city vibrant – it has the capacity to change over time…"

* Pat Page: "It is good to see something positive for a change."

* Jaime: "Just wanted to tell you that we look forward every week to your series. Don't change anything."

* Ruth Wells: "I have kept them all. … Very interesting are the various items listed but passed by for each letter."

* Gene Harvey: "When you start looking in detail at one city, you find out all the interesting things about it."

* Teresa Delgadillo: "(Your series) informs me about the city which I've lived in for 12 years. … I actually cut out your articles and go see some of the places you refer to that I don't know about. Second Street Bistro is probably the best … my boyfriend and I tried it and it was fantastic."

* Fred Goul: "You are doing a great job with the alphabet soup for Pomona. Suggest

you might change the ground rules for the second half of the Pomona alphabet and combine some of the letters. Besides, just how much material can you find with Q, V or X on Pomona?"

* Monique Ramirez: "I couldn't believe that nobody has written you since the letter I. Well, I just wanted to say that I love reading the 'Pomona A to Z' columns. I'm a third-generation native of Pomona."

* Bernice Alexander: "Although I live in Upland, I am enjoying your thoughts on Pomona."

* Danny McColgan: "Just wanted to say that I do like your 'Pomona A to Z' articles, being a second-generation Pomonan who started reading and delivering the Prog when I was a youngster in the early '60s."

On a personal note, the 10 responses this week were more than I'd received for all 13 "A to Z" columns combined. So I appreciate the support. This series might be the most fun I've had in 17 years in journalism.

Coming up: More of the same. I know it's a bad thing when John Kerry says it about a second Bush Administration, but I hope you'll enjoy N through Z anyway.

Especially Q, V and X.

After a four-week hiatus, "A to Z" returned to the newspaper, rested and refreshed. I had to acknowledge the grungier side of Pomona somehow, and devoting the letter N to the city's ubiquitous 99-cent stores was the way to go.

I asked Shawn Davis, an Arts Colony acquaintance and thrift store shopper, if she knew anybody who doted on 99-cent stores and she put me in touch with Willie Campos. Willie proved to be a hilarious tour guide, as you'll see.

Some of the discount stores in this column are gone, but they've been replaced by others, and in fact, discount stores have only become more mainstream in the past decade.

As for updates, the Inland Valley News is now based in Upland and the Butcher Paper is gone, although a monthly, bilingual community newspaper, La Nueva Voz, has been published out of Pomona since 2009. The NASA/JPL Center is scheduled to close in 2014. The Indian Hill Discount Store got a new sign circa 2007 identifying itself as the Indian Hill Discount Sore, a misspelling that's gone from astonishing to kind of sad the longer it remains. Sigh.

This column was published Nov. 14, 2004.

135

N is for 99-Cent Stores

'A to Z' blowout: Nothing here more than 99 cents!

Welcome back to "Pomona A to Z," in which we shine a spotlight on that venerable city's splendors, one letter at a time.

Today brings us to the letter N. In a nutshell, Pomona has numerous and nonpareil nominees. Numbered among them:

* Neon, still lighting up signs on many mid-century buildings in Pomona, often originated by Pomona's Williams Sign Co., in existence since 1930.

* NASA/JPL Educator Resource Center, established in the Village at Indian Hill by the two agencies to jet-propel science materials into Pomona schools.

* Newspapers, including the Inland Valley News, the area's only black-owned paper, and the Butcher Paper, a journal coming soon to the Arts Colony.

* National Hot Rod Association Museum at Fairplex, a nifty place for car nuts.

Not to be narrow-minded, but our N is none of the above. Instead, we'll recognize Pomona for its niche as the discount capital of the Inland Valley.

N is for 99 cents stores.

Shopper/hipster Willie Campos loads up at First Bargain 99 Cents, one of Pomona's numerous 99 cent stores.

True, this isn't the most glamorous honor, but discount shopping – think Indoor Swap Meet – is part of Pomona's identity.

Drive any major street here and you'll see some entrepreneur's variation on the 99

Cents Only chain's concept in almost every strip mall.

They have such names as 99 Cents Plus or, for people who want to save a penny, 98 Cents Plus. My personal favorite, Indian Hill Discount Store, bears the Chinese menu-like motto "Nothing Over 99 Cents Except Few."

My tour guide to this world was Willie Campos, a free spirit known in the Arts Colony for his love of cheap eats and treats.

"Everybody calls me Free Willie because I get everything for free," Campos told me. "I'm going to write a manual on how to live for free."

In the meantime, Campos led me around the 99 Cents Only Store on Holt Avenue, conveniently located within walking distance of his house. Visiting the chain store is one of the bright spots of his day.

"I know where every single item in this store is," Campos bragged.

He took me up and down the aisles, grabbing random items and shouting, "This would be $2.50 at Stater Brothers! Look at this. It's only 99 cents!"

Campos especially likes the Gourmet Fancy Foods section, where he sometimes picks up canned salmon. "I put this on bread with mayonnaise. It's better than tuna," he confided.

A 50-year-old with such disparate jobs as truck driver, mobile disc jockey and environmental engineer, Campos has been shopping at discount stores for a decade.

Although he first thought they were for poor people, he's come to believe they give consumers what they want: low, low prices. Grocery stores are cutting their own prices to compete, he said. Not that he goes there.

"I do all my shopping here!" Campos exclaimed.

He loaded a basket with two Gary Cooper DVDs in paper sleeves, three rolls of toilet paper, four Ginseng drinks (priced at two for 99 cents), a two-pack of John Morrell smoked sausage, a razor and three containers of shredded Gouda cheese.

Grand total: $10.33.

Outside the store, Campos wiped his forehead with a handkerchief.

"I'm exuberant with my great purchases," he admitted.

Nearby in the same strip mall is La Barata Discount Mart, a mom-and-pop outlet squeezed into a narrow storefront.

It's these sort of places that spawned the 99 Cents Only chain, Campos said, adding cultural anthropologist to his resume.

"They're mostly ethnic stores. They started off like this: Little stores with goofy stuff. You never know what you're going to find," he said.

Manager Hugo Munoz said La Barata has morphed into more of a swap meet with items of all prices.

"We have to compete with the big guys. You have to carry stuff they don't have," Munoz said.

From there, Campos and I hit a couple of locally owned under-a-buck stores. I drove him to First Bargain 99 Cents on Holt Avenue, which Campos admires for its wide aisles and 98-cent glass picture frames.

On South Garey we found 99 Cost Bargain, where a car outside bore a bumper sticker reading "I have a black belt in shopping."

Campos recalled that he once bought enough bargain-priced halogen lights at this store for his whole house.

As he had things to do and people to see, I drove him back to his car. (He'd saved money, I realized, by getting me to drive him around.)

"I can't wait to get home," Campos told me, thinking back on his morning's big purchase, "and put some Gouda on a baked potato!"

My dad is a sometime church organist and we had an organ in our house growing up (not that I do anything with music other than appreciate it). With this background, O was obvious: the biggest church organ in town.

Since publication, Pilgrim Church's organ has been rebuilt and reportedly sounds better than ever. And Mary Ferguson, the church organist featured in this piece, is still playing it.

In a minor update, the Opera Garage now has a nightclub above, not studios.

This column was published Nov. 28, 2004.

O is for Organ

'A to Z' pilgrimage keys in on old organ

By my oath! Today the alphabet obliges us to orate upon the letter O in "Pomona A to Z," our omnium-gatherum of Pomona's ostentatious, and occasionally *outré*, offerings.

To which outstanding O shall we pay obeisance? Overlooking others, here are two contenders:

* Opera Garage, the opera house at Fourth and Thomas that later housed the valley's first Cadillac dealership. Now the building has stores below and artists' studios above. Its car-sized elevator still works, by the way.

* Orange crate labels, 4,000 of which are in the collection of the Pomona Public Library. Access many of them online at http://content.ci.pomona.ca.us/databases.php

Obdurately, I've chosen another O. Observe as we compose an ode to Pomona's mightiest O: the organ at Pilgrim Congregational Church.

This baby is 102 years old and has

so many pipes, ranks and stops that by comparison, the Phantom of the Opera's organ sounds like a Wurlitzer.

Pilgrim Church is pretty stately itself. It's the red-brick, Gothic-style church at Garey Avenue and Pearl Street that dates to 1912 and covers a square block.

To demonstrate the organ's range for me one weekday afternoon, senior organist Mary Ferguson flipped the switches to set it humming to life.

The organ is housed near the altar but sunken behind a wooden screen so that Ferguson isn't visible from the pews.

Nestled behind the four-level keyboard, knobbed panels on either side, Ferguson resembled a pilot in a cockpit.

As she launched into "Praise God From Whom All Blessings Flow," the organ took off, rumbling and soaring.

"There's a lot of power there when you've got all that sound going," Ferguson said later.

Next she played part of a delicate Gregorian chant to show that the organ, like Sears, has a softer side.

Senior organist since 1986, Ferguson is called upon to play each Sunday and at weddings, funerals and church events.

Some couples planning weddings insist

they don't want an organ, a sentiment Ferguson doesn't understand.

"They must think of an electric organ or even relate them to funeral homes," Ferguson said. "But you don't want to come into a church and not have an organ."

No one's come into Pilgrim Congregational in more than a century and not had an organ.

Pilgrim Congregational organist Mary Ferguson is dwarfed by the 1902 organ and its largest pipes.

The church, founded in 1887, formed a "pipe organ club" in the 1890s to raise money. Its organ was ordered from Murray Harris Organ Builders of L.A. in a paired purchase with the local Methodist Church to bring down the price on two.

Pilgrim's organ debuted on March 4, 1902, and has been in use ever since. The Methodists' organ is history.

Marjorie Ough, the first organist, was still at the keyboards in 1942 at the organ's 40th anniversary, when expansions had more than doubled the original 780 pipes to 1,906.

When Japan surrendered, ending World War II, a special V-J Day service included a fitting organ prelude: Grieg's "Triumphal March."

Looming large in Pilgrim's history is Frank Cummings, its minister of music for a half-century. He presided over upgrades that brought the organ to its present size.

Ferguson learned the ropes under Cummings, who had been her music teacher at Pomona High and who retired from the church in 1985. He set high standards, ones she's still mindful of.

The 71-year-old makes the drive from Glendora at least three times a week to practice for Sunday's service, which typically has nine pieces of music.

"This congregation is used to good music, and appreciates it," Ferguson said.

That appreciation is quiet, this being church. But at a 2002 service to mark her 50 years of music involvement, Ferguson got, quite appropriately for today's theme, a standing O.

The organ now has 3,245 pipes, from the 16-foot monsters visible behind the altar to ones as small as a cigarette, plus 56 ranks and 72 stops.

Fund-raising is under way for a $238,000 rebuilding of the organ to restore its full sound. About 100 notes are dead and others are out of tune. Ferguson plays around them.

Even limping, the organ is like an orchestra, all in one instrument. It can mimic chimes, trumpets, a harp, strings and flutes. (No, there's no setting for rumba or cha-cha-cha.)

"It's a very versatile instrument," Ferguson said.

I decided not to ask her to play "Louie Louie."

As I've said, in this series I tried to touch on a wide swath of Pomona, including ethnicities. Thus, I was pleased to devote the letter P to an obscure but long-lived church serving the black community.

This column was published Dec. 12, 2004. Bear that in mind for a couple of references below to "today," which is long past.

P is for Primm

Pomona's small but proud church

Things have come to a pretty pass with "Pomona A to Z," which picks up with the letter P.

Among Pomona's plethora of P possibilities:

* Pan dulce at panaderias, the Mexican bakeries that are plentiful in Pomona.

* Phillips Mansion, the 1875 home of pioneer Louis Phillips, whose name graces Phillips Ranch and Phillips Boulevard.

* Presidential streets Lincoln, Roosevelt, McKinley, Madison, Adams, Jefferson, Garfield, Monroe and Buchanan.

* Porpoise statue depicted in mid-dive in an East Second Street fountain, installed as part of 1962's Pedestrian Mall.

* Picture postcards by Pomona photographer Burton Frasher Sr. (1888-1955). The Pomona Library has 5,000 of them, many viewable online at http://content.ci.pomona.ca.us/index_frasher.php

* Pomona College, which held its first

classes at White and Mission in 1888 before moving to Claremont – without changing its name – the next year. For entertainment value, it's hard to beat the plaque affixed to a rock that marks the historic college's birthplace, which is now Angelo's Burgers.

Which P to pick? What a pickle! But our P is yet another peak: Primm Tabernacle AME Church.

Dorothy Heard, left, and Johnnie Williams stand outside Primm Tabernace AME's former church building. Primm marks its 108th anniversary today.

Primm is no Pilgrim Congregational or First Baptist, the stately churches that consume entire city blocks in the heart of town, grand reminders of the days when Pomona was dubbed "City of Churches."

Primm is a modest complex along South Garey Avenue. Yet it has a history as noteworthy as its wealthier brethren.

The valley's first black church, it was pastored in the 1960s by the Rev. Cecil M. "Chip" Murray, who went on to become the best-known minister in Los Angeles.

The history is long, too. In fact, Primm is getting older all the time.

Its 40th anniversary fell in 1948, its 100th in 1998 and its 108th just six years later – today, as a matter of fact.

No, time isn't speeding up. Historians keep changing their mind on when the church started. More on this in a minute.

Today's service is planned for 10 a.m., followed by a ceremony and a soul food lunch.

Here's a capsule of milestones. Pomona's First AME – affiliated with the African Methodist Episcopal denomination – built a small church in 1908 at 10th and Thomas. The church adopted the Primm name in 1961, naming itself after an AME bishop, and moved to its current, larger quarters, a former Mormon church, in 1977.

The 1908 church still stands today as the home of a Baptist congregation. About the size of an apartment, the simple wooden building has been covered in gray stucco.

Next door is a small parsonage, and behind it is – historians take note – the original outhouse, used by Primm members until the 1977 move.

On a recent visit, two longtime church members reflected on the old days there.

Johnnie Williams, a member since 1963, remembers trying to sneak out of church early one day without the minister catching her. She was busted, she recalled with a laugh, when she left her Bible in the privy and had to go back for it.

Dorothy Heard joined the church in 1975. Despite a lifetime of churchgoing, Primm is where she finally felt saved.

"The place was small. Everybody had to sit close. We had to be close whether we wanted to or not," Heard said. "I miss this little church in a way."

Exactly when the little church began is hard to pin down. Records are sketchy, and newspapers virtually ignored the black church, as one might expect of that era.

City directories have surfaced with listings for "Methodist Church, African, corner Third and Olive" as far back as 1896, thus accounting for the 108th anniversary celebration today, event co-chairwoman Eleanor Duncan told me.

Who knows – with more research, the

110th anniversary could be next month.

There's no other information before 1909, but it's safe to conclude the church had just a handful of members, most of whom were probably citrus workers, domestics or janitors like other blacks of the day.

The church seems to have suffered shifting fortunes. Listings fell in and out of city directories over the first half of the 20th century, and a brief notice from 1947 in the Progress-Bulletin said the church was set to reopen.

Pomona's black population exploded in the 1960s, going from 800 in 1960 to 10,000 in 1970, setting the stage for the church's resurgence.

The Rev. Murray served in that era. He retired in fall 2004 as pastor of L.A.'s First AME, which he built from a small congregation to a must-stop for Democratic politicians.

Duncan and Williams are among those who remember Murray's 1964 to 1966 Pomona tenure, immediately after finishing his studies at the Claremont School of Theology.

"We were the first church he ever pastored," Duncan said. "In fact, he baptized my daughter (Eva), who's now an AME pastor. She was his first baptism."

Q turned out to be the hardest letter and the only one for which I had to fall back on something that no longer physically existed: the WW II-era Quartermaster Depot. (Although some of the buildings still stand.)

The quilt mentioned among the also-rans wouldn't have worked as a column subject without a gigantic photo to show each panel. Quinceaneras aren't unique to Pomona. Someone suggested Quality Thrift Store but that turned out to be in Montclair. And I wasn't going to pick Quizno's. Two years after "A to Z," I learned Pomona still had a quarter-midget racetrack. Shoot! Oh well, it's gone now anyway.

This column was published Dec. 26, 2004.

Q is for Quartermaster

Finding a Q for Pomona means turning to an old warhorse

"Pomona A to Z," my quixotic quest to document the city's quality, today reaches the letter Q, and you can imagine my qualms.

With readers' few Q suggestions mostly quartered in other cities, I was in a quandary, my qwerty keyboard quiet, until research – whew! – turned up examples of my quarry.

Let me queue up a quartet of possibilities:

* Quilt made for Pomona's 1988 centennial depicting structures from city history. Check it out on the second floor of City Hall. Can you identify each panel?

* Quest Academy, a private school on Phillips Boulevard serving students from grades three to 12.

* Quarter horse races at Fairplex Park during the L.A. County Fair.

* Quinceanera, the 15th-birthday celebration for Latinas, made possible by Pomona party, clothing and disc jockey

businesses.

Which Q will quantify Pomona's quintessence, you query? I hope you won't become quarrelsome when I say it's none of the above.

Instead, our Q is the Quartermaster Depot, the World War II-era name for what is now Cal Poly Pomona. Thanks to Betty Peters for the suggestion.

The depot was one of seven facilities in the nation where the U.S. military, to fight the Nazis, trained its secret weapon: horses.

Yes, horses.

Somehow we won the war anyway.

"It sounds like something out of the Civil War, doesn't it?" said Melissa Paul, curator of Cal Poly's Arabian Horse Library.

The Quartermaster's Remount Service was founded in 1775 to breed, train and supply horses to Army troops in the field and was still galloping along in the thick of the 20th century.

Mechanization was in its nascent stages in World War I, when 571,000 horses and mules carried supplies to U.S. troops.

The expectation was that World War II would be no different, Mary Jane Parkinson wrote in "The Kellogg Arabian Ranch: The First 60 Years," her history of the Cal Poly property.

U.S. Army Col. F.W. Koester, left, and his son, a lieutenant, pose in the Pomona Depot stables in January 1945.

American strategists learned the Germans had 791,000 horses, compared to our 750.

You've heard of the missile gap? This was a horse gap.

Spurred (har!) into action, the Remount Service looked for fresh horses and a site for a new depot in the West, which it found in good ol' Pomona on what had been cereal magnate W.K. Kellogg's 800-acre Arabian horse ranch.

The War Department took control in August 1943 and proved a better steward than the state university system, which had let the property decline after Kellogg donated it in 1932.

Under the Remount Service, horses again became the central mission and Sunday horse shows for the public continued.

Improvements were made, too. Block walls, landscaping and irrigation were installed by German and Italian prisoners of war, who were held at the Pomona fairgrounds.

No, they didn't eat rations of cotton candy and corn dogs.

Col. F.W. Koester, who had led the Army's War Dog center in San Carlos, was made Pomona's commanding officer, perhaps indicating that horses were a promotion from dogs.

But as it turned out, jeeps and trucks transported personnel and supplies in this war, not horses.

After the war, the Army got out of the horse business. It closed the Pomona Quartermaster Depot in June 1948.

"After more than four and a half years," Parkinson wrote of Kellogg's ranch, "the military air was gone; no more inspections from Quartermaster generals and colonels, no more military decorations ceremonies at the flagpole, no more Quartermaster insignia over the main entry to the stables, and no more salutes in the archways."

The ranch was nearly sold as surplus and its prized horses auctioned off until halted by a public outcry. The property, with the blessing of Kellogg, then 88, was deeded in 1949 to the state, which established what became Cal Poly.

Much of the wartime activity in Pomona remains a mystery.

"We have very little detail on what happened. We just don't have the records," said Paul, the library curator.

A sheaf of declassified documents a mere inch thick accounts for those five years. Author Parkinson managed to pry them from the National Archives under the Freedom of Information Act in 1990.

Among the tidbits deemed hush-hush for nearly a half-century: a 1942 inventory of Kellogg's 81 horses, with their names, and the one-page 1943 depot budget listing $36,340 in expenses, including the chief clerk's salary of $2,300.

Keep that on the QT.

The letter R proved a good excuse to recount how Pomona got its name, which came from the Roman goddess.

As for the runnerups, Robbie's, Red Hill Pizza and Randy's Records have all closed. Ruh-roh. Oh, and the "Jane Eyre" quote referred to at the start is actually "Readers, I married him." I had recently read the book and couldn't resist mentioning it.

This column was published Jan. 9, 2005, as "A to Z," which began back in July 2004, entered its second calendar year with a roar.

R is for Roman goddess

who brings classic touch to Pomona

To paraphrase "Jane Eyre": Readers, I'm at the letter R. OK, it's a loose paraphrase.

"Pomona A to Z," my recondite review of that city's raptures, today rests between Q and S. Which R should we recommend?

Let's reconnoiter in your ready room for a referendum:

* Rainbird Rainforest, a learning center at Cal Poly Pomona mimicking a rain forest and funded by the sprinkler company.

* Randy's Records, a vinyl album store on East Second Street, visited by many an out-of-town band at the Glass House.

* Red Hill Pizza, the eatery that spent 30 years in an old red barn on Holt before moving downtown. Try the lasagna.

* Robbie's, the downtown nightspot that in 1968 hosted a luncheon for Robert F. Kennedy, just days before his assassination.

* Reference department at the Library, always ready to respond to your research requests.

Well, I could go on and on – what about Repo Man Recovery? Rockwell Collins? the Donahoo's rooster? – but that might get repetitive.

Instead, let's stop roamin' and start Roman. Because our R is for Roman goddess, the deity for whom Pomona is named.

Until Los Angeles County redesigned its official seal in fall 2004, few realized its dominant image was the goddess Pomona in her flowing robes – a design created in 1957 by a Pomona native, artist Millard Sheets.

Tragically, Pomona got the heave-ho along with the seal's cross. County supervisors decided scrapping the cross but leaving the pagan goddess might send a weird message.

But who was Pomona, and how did a

Brought here from Italy in 1889, this statue of Pomona offers her marble bounty to library patrons.

Los Angeles suburb come to be named for a figure from Roman mythology?

"Not much is known about her," says Richard McKirahan, a professor of classics at – where else? – Pomona College.

She was a goddess, "but a minor one, not in the league of Jupiter or Venus," says McKirahan, noting that mentions of Pomona in myths are scant and sometimes contradictory.

Her sphere of influence was fruits, especially those that grow on trees. I forgot to ask whether that includes tomatoes.

"Her priest was the lowest ranking priest in the Roman hierarchy, which may mean that she was considered the humblest of the gods and goddesses," McKirahan says.

So Pomona's namesake is a goddess, but one with a public relations problem. Somehow that seems fitting.

The name came about like this. In 1875, real-estate investors from L.A. bought 2,500 acres out here for $10,000, then subdivided the land into lots for public auction.

They sponsored a contest to name the town.

Citrus nurseryman Solomon Gates, a Pennsylvania native who loved Greek and

Roman mythology, decided his entry would play off hopes that the town would become a horticultural paradise.

He feared the name would be too fancy, his son, Superior Court Judge Walter S. Gates, told the Historical Society in 1963.

But at a community meeting, contest judges declared: "Henceforth, our new settlement will be known as Pomona."

That's certainly better than the derisive nickname by which the settlement had been known: Monkey Town.

When the city incorporated on Jan. 6, 1888, Pomona was official. And catchy: At least eight other U.S. cities adopted the name.

Local images of the goddess abound. She was depicted on fruit crate labels. She's on the city seal, affixed to city vehicles, buildings and letterhead.

There are even modern twists. A wall-sized mural downtown features a Latino-tinged goddess.

More traditional is the version on display in the Pomona Library: a 5-foot-3 statue of Pomona carved from marble and shipped here from Italy more than a century ago.

As the Pomona Progress described the figure upon its arrival:

"It represents the goddess in the act of returning from the fruit harvest, the folds of her gown being filled with fruits, while in the hair about the brow are tastefully arranged small clusters of grapes."

An exact replica of a statue from antiquity, it was commissioned by the Rev. Charles F. Loop, a wealthy Episcopalian from Pomona. He saw the original while in Florence and thought a copy would make a dandy icon for his hometown.

It was presented on July 4, 1889, and has always been housed in the Library. Today, from inside her glass case, she keeps a watchful eye on the main floor.

"Most people just come by and look," library staffer Camilla Berger says. "But (a former staffer) told me that years ago, some people came in who worship Pomona."

Well, California is the land of fruits – and nuts.

Spadra was a natural choice for the letter S when I was writing this series. Not only is Spadra a crucial part of Pomona's origins, but people remain fascinated by the place, mostly because of its cemetery and the legends about frontier life and mysterious deaths. I've been in the library's special collections room more than once when some young person has come in to inquire politely about Spadra.

Mickey Gallivan of the Historical Society will be the first to tell you she plays up the drama because that's what people want to hear about Spadra. Too bad people persist in trespassing in the cemetery, which is private, and trashing the place. Not very respectful.

Among the runnerups, the world has stopped turning for Soap Opera Laundry, although the dryers still spin under the less dramatic name MXS Laundry.

This column was published Jan. 23, 2005.

S is for Spadra

Suddenly, 'Pomona A to Z' spotlights Spadra

Salaam, sahibs! "Pomona A to Z" today surveys the letter S for a symbol to sum up the city. There's such a surfeit, we won't have to scrounge.

So silence, please, as we sequester ourselves in our shacks and shanties, there to solemnly scan the scads of specimens:

* Sugar Shane Mosley, the boxer, and Suga Free, the rapper, who hail from Pomona. Sweet!

* The stylish stables built in 1909 for City Hall's horses in those pre-car days. They still stand at White and Monterey.

* Sacred Heart, St. Madeleine's and St. Joseph's, three churches serving the Catholic population.

* Special Collections, the room at the Public Library where you can research Pomona's past.

* Soap Opera Laundry, whose sign bears the image of a washing machine with TV-style rabbit ears.

Scintillating!

As you'd suspect, those only scratch the surface. We should also stop to salute Stan Selby, who led the Pomona Concert Band for an astounding 47 years until his death last November.

But our S is something different: Spadra.

A pioneer family's passing is marked in Spadra Cemetery, a slightly spooky remnant of the early Pomona community.

Now absorbed into west Pomona, Spadra lay roughly between today's Valley and Mission boulevards on either side of the 57 Freeway.

The village sprung up in 1866 along a stagecoach line, then began crumbling a decade later as the railroad passed it by. All that's left is the stately Phillips Mansion, which was built in 1875 and looks a lot like the house in "Psycho," and a rather sad cemetery.

Residents never saw the end coming. When the upstart settlement of Pomona began in 1875, Spadra's oldtimers derided it as "Monkey Town," for reasons that remain obscure.

"They just thought Pomona would never be anything," said Mickey Gallivan, president of the Historical Society of the Pomona Valley.

But it wasn't just Spadra that had a short life. So did an alarming number of people who lived there.

As "The Village That Died," a Historical Society booklet, puts it darkly: "The village of Spadra was characterized by murder, suicide and mysterious deaths."

Maybe S should be for s-s-s-spooky.

Many Spadra stories start at Billy Rubottom's inn, which is also where Spadra began. He'd bought 100 acres from Louis Phillips and set up shop along the Butterfield stage line.

To call Rubottom a colorful figure is like saying Shakespeare was a fair writer.

A rough frontiersman, he was wanted in his native Arkansas for killing two men with a knife. (I'm referring to Rubottom, not Shakespeare.)

And in El Monte, Rubottom shot his own son-in-law to death. Even more destructively, he's been blamed for importing California's first opossums.

Rubottom may have been the meanest man in Spadra, but he had competition – even from a man of the cloth.

In 1872, the Rev. William Standifer, a farmer, angrily confronted the town constable, knocking him down twice. A bullet in the shoulder from the constable's gun only made Standifer madder. So the next bullet found the minister's heart.

Spadra also saw a murder-suicide between two lovers and an ex-con stabbed to death by his brother-in-law, among other untimely demises. As recently as this month, January 2005, a ghostly figure has been reported in the Phillips Mansion.

The cemetery in Spadra has 212 graves, officially.

If you were killed in a barfight at Rubottom's for, say, cheating at cards, "the rumor is they just dragged you off to the cemetery and buried you," Gallivan said. "So there are probably more than 212 people buried there."

The name Spadra, by the way, was stolen by Rubottom from his hometown in Arkansas. According to Gloria Ricci Lathrop's "Pomona: A Centennial," though, it was his second choice.

The valley was already known as San Jose from its days under Spanish rule. But Rubottom's application for a post office by that name was rejected, because California already had a San Jose.

He succeeded with the name Spadra. We know it as Spah-dra, although the Arkansas pronunciation is said to be Spay-dra.

Opened in 1868, the Spadra post office was among the first half-dozen in California. The village was off to a good start.

Settled mostly by poor families fleeing the South, bustling Spadra soon had a school, a major road, warehouses for trade goods, three stores and two blacksmiths. All it lacked was a Starbucks.

Unfortunately, it soon lacked more than that. While Southern Pacific extended its line eastward to Spadra in 1874, by the next year the line went as far as Colton.

The train didn't stop in Spadra anymore, and almost no one else did, either.

So long, Spadra.

Somewhere along the line I'd heard Shelton's was a cult favorite and thus its product, turkeys, was tailor-made for the letter T.

Of the runnerups, the trompe l'oeil *paintings were nixed because, newspaper space being at a premium, it was hard enough for me to get one photo into print, much less two. There was also a lobbying effort (an e-mail or two) by the Tony's French Dips people, who contacted me several letters in advance to make a pitch. Tony's would have been worthy too; it was spotlighted in one of my 2013 columns.*

This column was published Feb. 6, 2005.

T is for Turkeys

Calling today's 'A to Z' column a turkey is fair game

For Super Bowl Sunday, "Pomona A to Z" touches down on T.

Yes, this series' trajectory means it's time to pay tribute to the alphabet's 20th letter.

Let me tell you, Pomona is a tableau that's teeming with T's, each contributing to the texture of that tremendous town, each a triumph that ought to be trumpeted.

Tingle at these tidbits:

* Twinkies at the L.A. County Fair — deep-fried, of course.

* *Trompe l'oeil* ("trick of the eye") murals: one on the wall of a city parking lot at Second and Garey and another on the Sign-Wize office at Park and Monterey.

* Totem pole towering in the front yard of the home at Arrow Highway and Wilkie Drive.

* Two Thai restaurants in the same block of South Indian Hill: Sanamluang and Mix Bowl. They're tip-top.

* Todd Memorial Chapel, a funeral home owned and operated by the same family since 1907.

* Tony's French Dips, a Police Department favorite that's served sandwiches since 1958. Cook Angie Campos has been dipping for three decades.

* Tacos, tortas and tortillas at Tropical Mexico (often known as Trop Mex) and other traditional taquerias.

Treasures all! And now that you've got the thrust of my theme, let me thrill you by revealing the T we're tackling:

Turkeys from Shelton's Poultry.

Getting a turkey from Shelton's is an Inland Valley tradition. As Thanksgiving approaches, there's often a line out the front door and around the corner for Ben Franklin's favorite bird.

"It's a social event," said chief financial officer Ruth Flanagan, whose family owns Shelton's.

Some customers have been coming for decades, and they love to share their memories of past purchases – talking turkey, as it were – with the staff.

Rich Havlena of Montclair has been buying Shelton's turkeys for 30 years.

"You can taste the difference," the retired phone company man, 62, told me.

"And you can't hardly screw 'em up."

Good news for once-a-year turkey chefs everywhere.

Fresh turkey wasn't such a rare commodity in the olden days. The Pomona valley once had five turkey ranches, until they were gobbled up (har!) for development.

The bird is the word at Shelton's, where CEO Gary Flanagan holds a frozen turkey for your inspection.

Shelton's began in 1924, when newlyweds Margaret and O.J. Shelton got a unique wedding present: two turkeys. Hey, it beats another blender.

The couple bred their hen and tom and later began selling turkeys for meat. They had a ranch of about 15 acres at Franklin and San Antonio avenues, near today's Simons Middle School.

O.J. Shelton died and in 1969 so did Fred, their son – the product of their personal breeding program.

Egg distributor Ken Flanagan and his family bought the business from Margaret that year. The Pomona natives have owned it ever since. Ken is retired, but four Flanagan sons and a sister-in-law share the business equally.

Shelton's got out of the ranching business in 1970, when a farm in the middle of a suburb had become impractical.

"You need to be in a rural area. This isn't rural anymore," CEO Gary Flanagan said.

Turkeys are now raised in Fresno and slaughtered in Turlock, then shipped south. The Pomona facility on Loranne Avenue does cutting, boning and packaging, as well as retail sales.

Shelton's sells 150,000 turkeys a year and 650,000 chickens, for $15 million in gross revenue – a decent output, but a far cry from Foster Farms.

"We've survived because we're a niche market," Gary Flanagan told me.

All Shelton's turkeys and chickens are free range, meaning they're raised outdoors and get more exercise, Flanagan said. Their food is natural and they aren't given any chemicals.

As a company motto goes: "Our chickens don't do drugs."

(I believe their turkeys are warned: "Just gobble no.")

Natural food stores and specialty markets such as Whole Foods and Wolfe's in Claremont stock Shelton's products, which include broth, canned chili and frozen entrees.

"We're kind of the Tyson's of the natural food business," Flanagan said. "We sell natural food products in all 50 states."

Some high-end restaurants, notably L.A.'s venerable Pacific Dining Car, serve Shelton's chicken.

To my knowledge, Shelton's did not supply any turkeys to "WKRP in Cincinnati" sitcom character Arthur Carlson for his radio station's ill-fated Thanksgiving promotion.

You may recall how a shopping center was bombed with live turkeys from a helicopter, leading to Hindenburg-like chaos.

"As God is my witness," a shaken Carlson said later, in a classic moment of television, "I thought turkeys could fly."

My U choice was unknown until the day I finally took at look at that stone marker outside Joey's BBQ. When I read the inscription commemorating the nearby underpass, I laughed out loud there on the street corner. Granted, underpasses aren't unique to Pomona – but stone markers for underpasses may be!

This column was published Feb. 20, 2005.

U is for Underpass

Pomona underpass was urgent undertaking for 76 years

It's unnerving, but "Pomona A to Z," my unabashedly upbeat ode to the city's unplumbed depths, is up to the letter U.

Examples aren't ubiquitous, but Pomona does have some unforgettable U runnerups with which you may be unacquainted:

* Underground art galleries in the basement of the Prog and Founders buildings downtown: Gallery 57 Underground, SCA Gallery and SoHo Gallery.

* U Pick U Save Auto Dismantling on East Mission, worth a U-turn by those looking for a replacement hubcap or side mirror.

* Unistar Foods, which provides meat and poultry to Filipino American restaurants and markets throughout Southern California.

Uplifting, eh? However, the U that deserves a chorus of ululation is unique –

193

and admittedly unpromising.

It's the Garey Avenue underpass.

(That's underpass, not underpants.)

Each day, thousands of motorists pass below the railroad tracks downtown without a second thought.

But it wasn't always this way. Waiting from a few minutes to a half-hour for a train to pass was once a daily occurrence.

Showing that government moves even slower than trains, the problem existed for eight decades before anything was done.

In 1887, the Progress-Bulletin editorialized:

"The railroad crossing at Garey Avenue was blocked last Monday forenoon for a considerable length of time by a freight train, causing no little annoyance and delay to passing to and fro of teams. That is an annoyance that should be abated at once."

"Teams," by the way, referred to horse-drawn wagons. Told you this was an age-old problem.

As Pomona grew, there was talk of building underpasses at the Garey, White and Towne rail crossings. Efforts intensified after July 15, 1948, when traffic was blockaded at noon for a half-hour, then at 1:30 p.m. for another half-hour.

From the Pomona Progress-Bulletin files comes this photo and caption from July 29, 1961: "LAST STOP - Railroad gates will be lowered for the last time this weekend to stop traffic at the Garey Avenue crossing. The crossing will be blocked off Monday before ground-breaking at 11 a.m. for a new underpass."

Road rage, anyone?

As if reaching across the years to help me write today's U-themed column, Southern Pacific passenger agent William Campbell told the Progress-Bulletin the incidents were "unfortunate and unavoidable."

Enter Fred Sharp. Hired in 1949 as Pomona's first city administrator, Sharp set about preparing the city for the future. Storm drains, a county courthouse and a new Civic Center were among his achievements before retiring in 1974.

So were rail crossings.

"People were getting killed on the railroad tracks ... There was no program in California for (underpass construction). We had to go to court to force the railroads to cooperate. They claimed they were here first," Sharp recalled in a 1985 interview.

By the late 1950s, railroads were required by state law to cough up money for grade separations. A state fund was set up to provide matching funds for qualifying projects.

Thanks to Pomona's lobbying, Garey, White and Towne made the cut. Pomona voters overwhelmingly passed a $1.5 million bond issue to raise the city's share – 30 percent – of the $5.3 million needed.

"It was a great effort. And the business community was strongly behind it," Ora Lampman, hired in 1962 as a city engineer, told me recently.

Towne and White were done first. Construction on Garey began in August 1961. It turned into a nightmare, dragging on for two years because of its complexity.

Vehicle traffic was rerouted and temporary trestles were built to carry the trains.

Some 6,000 truckloads of dirt were hauled off. Then work began on the

110-foot-wide bridge, which supported three sets of tracks and two lanes of First Street.

Like an omelet, you can't create a grade separation without breaking a few eggs. Did I really just type that? Pomona had to demolish a block of First Street on the west side of Garey as well as the 1914 Union Pacific depot.

Further setting this undercrossing apart is what may be the most unusual public works plaque in the Inland Valley.

I'm referring to a 6-foot stone marker rising nobly at the corner of Second and Garey, right outside a barbecue joint.

When I saw this grand monument to a humble underpass, I knew it was worthy of "Pomona A to Z."

Anyway, on Aug. 15, 1963 – some 76 years after the 1887 editorial – Pomona held a lavish dedication for the underpass.

Some 1,000 people heard County Supervisor Frank Bonelli praise Pomona for perseverance "that is second to none."

Perseverance that was tested again – just to sit through all the speeches.

After a monthlong break for reasons I can't recall – vacation? deadline problems? other news crowding to get into my column? – "A to Z" returned to print with the letter V.

I was happy to write about the Vietnamese community, fulfilling my goal of writing about the main ethnic groups in the city. There is still a vital Vietnamese presence in Pomona, and the restaurant Pho Vi opened at Third and Thomas streets downtown. The only update to this piece is that the Vault nightclub, one of the runnerups, is gone.

This column was published March 27, 2005.

V is for Vietnamese

'A to Z' veers toward topic you won't pho-get

Filling a vacuum, my virtuous venture "Pomona A to Z" returns today to venerate that village's virtues (while avoiding its vices).

Yes, we're visiting the letter V, or vice versa. Which V best reflects the voodoo that Pomona does so well?

After vigorously vetting or vetoing a vast variety of V's, I've voted for these vignettes, all vis-a-vis V:

* Veterinary school at the Western University of Health Sciences. Amazingly, it's the only one in Southern California, as well as the only one in the nation headed by a woman.

* Vintage clothing from La Bomba, which dresses visiting rock stars and various locals.

* The Vault nightclub, housed in the 1925 First National Bank building, hence the name.

* Pioneering landowner Ricardo Vejar, who in 1837 co-owned the entire Pomona Valley. A footnote: The city bought 22 acres

from his estate in 1922 to launch the L.A. County Fair.

Va-va-voom! Why, these V's practically give me vertigo.

Yet I hope it won't vex you to learn that our V is a different indicator of Pomona's vitality. Our V gives voice to a community that's very valuable: the Vietnamese.

After the April 30, 1975 fall of Saigon to the North Vietnamese – 30 years ago next month – many Vietnamese fled communism and misery by cramming themselves valiantly into rickety wooden boats for the vagaries of a sea voyage to neighboring countries for repatriation.

Some 125,000 were accepted as refugees by the United States that year, the vanguard of more than 270,000 that followed by 1982, gaining the world's sympathy.

A Vietnamese couple eat at Pho USA, one of several Vietnamese businesses along Pomona's East Holt Avenue. The gentleman seems to have handled his pho better than David Allen did at another restaurant.

Many settled in Orange County, but impressive numbers ended up in the Inland Valley. They're concentrated in Pomona, where an estimated 10,000 live.

You may not even know they're there, as the community is less visible than Pomona's majority Latino population.

But a stretch of East Holt Avenue shows their presence. Hoa Binh is a market with Asian food and produce, as well as an eye-opening array of fresh fish. Asian characters can be seen on numerous storefronts.

Rather than experience this vicariously, I invited Diep Fintland to lunch. A real estate broker, she is a leader among local Vietnamese. We met at a popular restaurant, Pho Express, for my inaugural Vietnamese meal.

A type of soup, pho is pronounced "fuh." (Now that you're familiar with pho, no one can call you a fuddy-duddy.)

"Pho, it's like pancakes for Americans. Usually it's for breakfast, but you can eat it 24 hours," Fintland said.

My bowl of Pho Tai – broth, rice noodles and rare steak – was delicious, albeit virtually impossible to eat.

The long, pasta-like noodles are meant to be eaten with chopsticks. I'm sure I could have done this if I'd had two hours – or the

24 hours Fintland mentioned – but after I fumbled around a while, owner Hoa Phan brought me a fork.

She and Fintland exchanged amused comments in Vietnamese about my struggle, some of which Fintland translated.

"You're eating it like spaghetti!" Fintland joked as I twirled the noodles against my soup spoon with my fork.

Fintland, meanwhile, plucked the thin slices of beef from her pho and expertly rolled them into tubes, all with her chopsticks, for dipping into a saucer of spicy liquid. I shakily carried mine over flat with chopsticks or my fork.

I ate one-third of my pho before deciding to phogeddaboudit.

Much easier to eat, and just as tasty, were Cha Gio, a meaty eggroll wrapped in lettuce, and Phan Tau Hu Ky, crispy cubes of deep-fried tofu around shrimp paste. Now that's eatin'!

The restaurant had a bustling lunch crowd of Vietnamese, Latinos and Caucasians. It re-opened in fall 2004 after several years as Pho 54 under different hands.

Phan's son, Timmy Nguyen, who runs the restaurant, says his family had a hard life in Vietnam before coming here as refugees in 1983.

"That's what has made me successful in the U.S. I don't take anything for granted," said Nguyen, 35, who sold cars for 11 years before helping his mother open the restaurant. He added later: "I adore America."

Fintland came here in 1967 – by commercial plane – after high school to join a sister who'd married a serviceman. Their father was killed by the Communists when Fintland was 2.

She and her husband, whom she met in Bakersfield, have lived in Pomona since 1977.

Madelenna Lai and Fintland founded the Pomona organization Vietnamese Cultural House in 1997 to help preserve their roots. In 2002 they sponsored a Rose Parade float, in the shape of a boat, as a way to thank Americans for taking their people in.

"Freedom. A lot of people take it for granted," Fintland observed.

There's a lot of veracity in that.

For W, I focused on a whole neighborhood, one that has a certain fascination for midcentury architecture buffs because of its tracts designed by Cliff May, creator of the ranch home. Oh, and the two people who run Westmont Hardware turned out to be a couple of authentic characters and well worth meeting. They retired in 2013 and closed the store.

Willie White, numbered among the W candidates, died in 2011 at age 75, but his name lives on at Willie White Park.

One improvement anticipated in this column has partly come to pass: a Mission Boulevard interchange opened in 2011, even if plans to turn the Corona Expressway, also known as the 71, into a full-fledged freeway through Pomona are still on the horizon.

This column was published April 10, 2005.

W is for Westmont

'Pomona A to Z' watches over Westmont

Welcome! "Pomona A to Z" today wades into the letter W, as we seek to become well-informed about Pomona, and not in a willy-nilly way.

To which W shall we bear witness? Try not to become weepy as I wistfully whisper of these wonders:

* Willie White, a former councilman, youth advocate and current neighborhood activist whose name is on a park.

* Winternationals, the largest drag-racing event in the world.

* Wilton Heights, a neighborhood of Craftsman bungalows and stately homes designated as a city historic district.

* Western University of Health Sciences, a school of osteopathic medicine that now occupies much of East Second Street, including the old Buffum's department store.

Wild!

As is my wont, though, our W is

different: Westmont.

That's the western Pomona neighborhood that exemplified post-World War II optimism. Some 1,200 homes sprang up from 1946 to 1954, along with a shopping center, park, community center, elementary school and church.

With a little imagination, you could picture the superfamily from "The Incredibles" here. Homes along Wright and

Not to hammer you over the head, but Westmont Hardware is one of several Westmont-centric buildings in the Westmont neighborhood.

Denison streets have a similar, if smaller-scale, look to the movie: open floor plans, floor-to-ceiling windows, clean lines and side patios.

And take a gander at Westmont

Community Center, Westmont Elementary or Westmont United Methodist Church, all on West Ninth Street. Is that Elastigirl and the kids driving (or flying) by?

Westmont got its start when home builder Edwin A. Tomlin began work on newly annexed land south of today's Mission Boulevard and bisected by today's Corona Expressway.

Most of his homes were standard stuff for returning GIs, but then Tomlin got experimental, hiring architect Arthur Lawrence Millier to design 50 affordable modern homes. Another 100 were prefab modern homes by Cliff May and Chris Choate.

May and Choate's work was described by House and Home magazine as "almost the first low-cost house to offer the kind of California living everybody back East imagines all Californians enjoy."

Maybe W should be for "whoa."

Bruce Emerton has become a neighborhood archivist and booster since buying his home in 1995 for $130,000. He painstakingly restored his 1954 May home to its original look.

An art and architecture librarian at Cal Poly Pomona, Emerton drove me around on Wednesday, pointing out nice homes and shaking his head over ill-advised remodeling.

"A lot of them have been stuccoed and bastardized," Emerton admitted. "A few are in good shape. Even a lot of ones that are messed up could be brought back."

Speaking of messed up homes, people still talk about the 1982 city-sanctioned dynamite blast to close a dangerous cave in the Westmont Hills behind the neighborhood.

Fifteen homes were blown off their foundation and more than 500 were damaged. Oopsie!

A commemorative T-shirt quoting "Butch Cassidy and the Sundance Kid" put it this way: "Think Ya Used Enough Dynamite There, Butch?"

Westmont, though, is best remembered as home to General Dynamics, a missile factory that employed 13,000 at its peak. The plant opened in 1953 as Convair and closed in the early 1990s, the victim of Southern California aerospace cutbacks.

In its heyday, the plant produced missiles with such fun-lovin' names as Red Eye, Mauler, Terrier and Advanced Terrier. Does Jack Russell know about this?

Unlike General Dynamics, one neighborhood icon remains. Westmont Hardware is a cozy store dating to 1949 that's hanging on in this era of Home Depot and Lowe's.

It has just two employees: owners Russell Riedel and Patsy Koenig.

Riedel was hired at the store out of high school in 1967 and has been there ever since, buying it in 1989 from its second owner. He remembers General Dynamics employees crossing Mission Boulevard "like herds of cattle" on lunch breaks, then the bad times later.

Things are more stable now. When the expressway becomes a freeway with a Mission interchange, big changes will come.

"I've been hearing about it 30 years," said Riedel, who's not exactly holding his breath.

Well, that's the story of Westmont.

Was I too wordy?

As you can imagine, finding an X for "A to Z" was exceedingly difficult. (Although writing the intro was fun.)

Xochimilco was one of Pomona's longest-lived Mexican restaurants – perhaps only Tropical Mexico was older – but a few months after publication, Xochimilco expired. Its replacement, Mariscos Ensenada No. 5, isn't bad at all, and it may be superior.

But a couple of generations of diners enjoyed Xochimilco and its colorful exterior mural, so this piece has value, perhaps, as history. It was published April 24, 2005.

In 2011, I visited the real Xochimilco in Mexico, plying the canals in a flat-bottomed boat, a trajinera. It's a memory I'll always connect to a little restaurant in Pomona.

X is for Xochimilco

X marks the dining spot in 'Pomona A to Z'

Step away from your Xbox and turn down your X record! Your full attention is needed for "Pomona A to Z," my love letter of X's and O's for Pomona, as I embrace the letter X.

From Xenia, Ohio, to Xian, China, readers are wondering how yours truly, the Inland Valley's answer to Xenophon, will find an X in Pomona.

The answer: With X-tra difficulty. To paraphrase the country song, all my X's are in Texas, not Pomona.

Still, even if X candidates aren't exactly springing up through xenogenesis, we can luxuriate in these runner-ups:

* X-rays at Pomona Valley Hospital Medical Center, where the radiology department handled more than 155,000 x-citing procedures in 2004.

* "X-Files," which filmed its Jan. 13, 2002 episode, in which Agent Doggett is in a Mexican jail with amnesia, in the 500 block of West Second Street. A Virgin Mary painting done for the shoot is still visible on a brick wall.

* The businesses Xcessories N Things, Xemco Inc., Xepa Car Wash, Xiomara Beauty Salon, XLent Technology and – hold onto your hat – Xochiquetzal Dance Studio.

X-cellent! With this bounty, it must be Xmas.

Yet the X in my little xylograph is a different choice. Before you start nagging me like Socrates' wife Xanthippe, here it is: Xochimilco Mexican Restaurant.

Opened in November 1969 and still in the same minimall at Indian Hill and Holt, Xochimilco (pronounced "So-chee-MEEL-co") is one of Pomona's oldest Mexican eateries.

"People used to line up 20 minutes or a half hour outside because there weren't that many Mexican restaurants," said waitress Elsie Alvarez, who grew up nearby.

It's been an oasis of stability in a changing world. The name, address, recipes, much of the decor and even the phone number have stayed constant.

"Oasis" is appropriate because the real Xochimilco is a garden and series of canals outside Mexico City known as "Mexico's own Venice."

Restaurant founder Carroll Gauslin

loved vacationing in Xochimilco, Alvarez said. But he wasn't from Mexico.

This carved toucan adds to the atmosphere inside Xochimilco Mexican Restaurant, where Yesenia Raygoza and Blu Torres ate lunch last week.

According to the story on a past menu, Gauslin was raised in New Mexico and Texas, where he picked up a love for chiles. He created the recipes for Xochimilco himself. A friendly, well-liked man, he married one of his waitresses, Dolores.

After his death, she kept the restaurant for a spell, then sold it in October 2001 to Carlos Argueta. Since May 2004 it's been in the hands of David Gutierrez, only the third owner in the restaurant's 35-year history.

Xochimilco has regulars who've been coming for years, first with their parents and now as adults.

Cathy Goring is one of them. She e-mailed to suggest I write about the place, which she's been frequenting pretty much since it opened. So I invited her to lunch.

"I grew up a few blocks from here. We used to come here once a month when I was growing up," Goring told me. Those were the days when the nearby mall, now the Indoor Swap Meet, had a Sears and a Zody's Discount Department Store.

She recalled Xochimilco's decor as being largely the same – quirky but memorable.

Bird cages with carved birds still hang from the ceiling. ("I Know Why the Caged Fake Bird Doesn't Sing"?) Some diners sit under a shingled covering or a trellis. Odd, but nice.

The upholstered chairs and the beautifully tiled tables are said to have been brought from Mexico by Gauslin.

But the food is key. An online dining review says that "generations have enjoyed the chile rellenos," and Goring said they're among her favorites too. I tried one and liked it.

"It's always good to come back and see the food is just as good as it used to be,"

Goring said of her enchilada plate. "That was my fear when it changed hands, that the recipes would change."

One reason they didn't is that Serafin Juarez was the cook from the beginning until just two months ago, when he retired.

The original written recipes are still used, said manager Blanca Linebaugh, who is Gutierrez's sister.

"I have them," Linebaugh said. "And I make sure we're following them."

She might go one step further and make a Xerox.

Here we are at the penultimate letter! Yellow Cab made a pitch to be the letter Y, telling me they've got several vintage taxis in their Pomona yard, but since that's not open to the general public, I opted to go with the YMCA. Besides, the Y is one of the most prominent buildings in Pomona – even if, as noted below, a lot of people don't realize it houses a Y.

As of 2012, it no longer does. The Y moved within Pomona to 1460 E. Holt Ave. and its former headquarters sold in 2013, a move likely to mean continued life for the stately building.

Also, Yesteryears, one of the runnerups, is no longer in business.

This column was published June 12, 2005.

Y is for YMCA

This 'A to Z' should have no one asking Y

Yay! Today – not yesterday – "Pomona A to Z" yields the floor to the letter Y.

By any yardstick, Pomona has great examples of Y's. Oh, you think I'm a yo-yo? Then pay attention to this yarn.

Yes, stop yammering on your cell phone, eating yogurt and adjusting your yarmulke! Whether your chromosomes are X or Y, just eye this list of Y's, yonder:

* Yesteryears nightclub on West Second Street, one of the Arts Colony's live music venues.

* Yamamotoyama of Orient, maker of fine Japanese teas, located in a west Pomona industrial park.

* Yellow Cab, which began as City Transit in 1926 at Main and Second and now serves the entire Pomona valley with taxis and paratransit buses.

Yowza!

Anyway, yada yada yada, let's just go to our Y.

The literal Y. The YMCA.

One of the most recognizable buildings in Pomona, the red-bricked YMCA stands at 350 N. Garey Ave., where it takes up most of a block.

"Young man, there's a place you can go...": Pomona's historic, hopping YMCA.

"There's a lot of brick recognition," quips J.J. Diaz-Ceja, the membership fitness director. "Everybody walks by and recognizes the brick."

Yet not everybody knows it's a Y, despite the modest neon sign on the building's corner.

"One question I often get from people is, 'How long has this been a YMCA?' " Diaz-Ceja says.

Try "forever."

Pomona began a fund-raising campaign for the stately, Mission-style building soon after the end of World War I.

Architect Robert Orr's design, notable for its arched windows, was described in a 1919 fund-raising appeal as having been "pronounced of singular beauty and usefulness by the ablest YMCA experts of the Pacific Coast."

A suitably impressed public contributed $300,000, all the more startling in a city of just 18,000.

Built on the site of the Palomares Hotel, which was lost to fire in 1912, the YMCA was dedicated in April 1922 with a speech by Gov. William Stephens. More than 1,000 citizens turned out.

As an orator from Iowa College put it: "Let this building be dedicated to brotherliness. Let us all join hands that we might feel the thrill of the Almighty, that men may grow up among brotherhood and achieve brotherhood. Keep yourselves related to a center of brotherhood."

Oh, brother.

The YMCA – the initials stand for Young Men's Christian Association – started in England in 1844 as an attempt to apply Christian principles to everyday problems. It then spread to the United States.

Pomona's chapter began in 1884 as a reading room and job-placement service. It soon faded until its revival in 1919, according to a history by Steven Escher.

As you'd expect, a lot of changes have occurred over the past 83 years.

First limited to men and boys, the Y allowed women and girls to become members in 1949. With no YWCA in town, they had been auxiliary members previously.

The auditorium, initially devoted to Bible study, was turned into a gym in 1940 due to growing demand for space. A $300,000 wing was added in 1958, expanding the building further.

When I visited last week, a pickup basketball game was going on in the gym. High above were the original stained glass windows – handy for anyone praying to make that jump shot.

Today's Y has aerobics classes, weight machines and child care. While teens were the early focus, the Y now caters more to families.

Although Christian principles remain the organization's bedrock, "anyone can join the YMCA," Diaz-Ceja emphasizes.

Anyone from yokel to yacht dweller, I'm sure. Call (909) 623-6433 for membership details, or drop by for a tour.

The Y, by the by, is booming. Since the hiring of Phyllis Murphy as general director and CEO in 2001, the Y has grown from an anemic 400 members to nearly 1,200.

I enjoyed the chance to see the place. Although, admittedly, I was disappointed not to find any Village People.

One highlight was the indoor pool. Twenty yards long, the pool has the Y's original logo laid into the aqua tile.

This is where generations of Pomona children learned to swim or took their Boy Scout swimming test. Today, it's also used for lap swimming and aquatic aerobics.

"Unbelievable as it may seem, this is the original tile," Diaz-Ceja brags.

The building was made a state landmark in 1985 and a national landmark in 1986.

After my visit, I could see Y.

Well, here we are at the end. I had the topic for Z picked far in advance, relishing the neatness of ending the series the way it began. People kept asking what Z would be but I think the only person I told was Mickey Gallivan, and that's only because I interviewed her for it.

Among the runnerups, zarzeula *is no longer sung in Pomona, alas, and if you need a bail bond, the defunct Zzooms will be of no help. (You could try Aladdin, at the other end of the alphabet.)*

Dorothy Ziolkowski died in 2005, not long before this column was published. One of her daughters later told me her mother, a very proud Pomonan, would have loved the mention. That being the case, I'll dedicate Z to her memory.

This column was published June 19, 2005.

Z is for Zanja

You'll really dig Pomona's letter Z

Zounds! "Pomona A to Z," which began in this space last (gulp) July 18, today finally reaches the 26th letter: Z.

Yes, it's been a zigzag path to Z, but now we're at the zenith of the "A to Z" ziggurat!

Here we can sip zinfandel, munch on zwieback and dance to zydeco music, while reminiscing about the Z Channel and musing about the zeitgeist.

But let's hold the zeal until Z is revealed.

Admittedly, my job would be a lot easier if Pomona had a zoo. But to my surprise, the city is zaftig with Z's:

* *Zarzuela*, or Spanish musical theater, performed annually at Ganesha Park by (whoa!) the L.A. Opera.

* Jim Zorn, a former quarterback for the Seattle Seahawks who set 10 school records in football at Cal Poly Pomona.

* Tom Zasadzinski, Cal Poly Pomona's official photographer.

* Dorothy Ziolkowski, a hard-workin' volunteer for the Friends of the Pomona

Library.

* Zzooms Bail Bonds, located near the police station, the better to zoom in to get you out.

Blow me down with a zephyr!

Our Z, of course, is none of these. Admittedly obscure, this Z was there at the start of Pomona, and it's still there today.

It's *zanja*.

(No, not ganja, which was there at the start of Jamaica, and is still there today – *zanja*.)

Pronounced "sahn-ha," this was the stone-lined ditch that carried water to Pomona's first settlements.

It was dug beginning in 1840 to bring water from San Jose Creek to the adobes for irrigation and personal use.

"It was the first water system," says Mickey Gallivan, president of the Historical Society.

Short segments still exist outside the three remaining adobes: La Casa Primera and Palomares Adobe, which are public, and Alvarado Adobe, which is privately owned.

I learned about the *zanja* when I visited La Casa Primera (1569 N. Park) for the letter A. Docent Luis Guerrero showed me the ditch in the back.

This zanja, or ditch, behind La Casa Primera carried water to Pomona's original settlers. Zowie!

Going out the way "A to Z" came in, we're back to the beginnings of Pomona.

Two ranchers, Ygnacio Palomares and Ricardo Vejar, were given title to 15,000 acres of former mission land in 1837, when California was still part of Mexico.

Vejar settled in the south. Palomares

took the north, building La Casa Primera, the first house in the Pomona Valley.

He soon had a neighbor. He invited his cousin, Ygnacio Alvarado, to build a house a stone's throw away.

(Archaeological note: This stone has not been found.)

Alvarado dug the *zanja* in 1840. It was enlarged as more settlers moved in and needed water, according to an 1888 report by the state engineer.

Palomares moved to a new, larger home in 1854, now known as Palomares Adobe (491 E. Arrow Highway), and a *zanja* was dug there, too.

A drought in the early 1860s killed thousands of cattle in California, making vast ranches hard to sustain. Vejar borrowed money at predatory rates and lost his holdings.

Palomares' widow sold 2,000 acres of the homestead in 1874 for $8 an acre to two investors. The sale spelled an end to the Rancho San Jose days – but paved the way for Pomona!

Investors sold off lots for the fledgling city, which incorporated in 1888 with a population of 3,500.

Progress eventually zonked the *zanjas*.

"The little ditch that had brought water

from San Antonio *Canon* across the sandy waste lands became tunnels and pipe lines and irrigating ditches ..." wrote Bess Adams Garner and Miriam Colcord Post in a Historical Society pamphlet.

In L.A., a *zanja* resurfaced, literally, in March 2005. The *Zanja Madre* ("Mother Ditch"), the city's primary water source from 1781 to 1904, was discovered by the Metropolitan Transportation Authority, which was grading land for a rail line.

The 4-foot-wide, brick-lined ditch was quickly reburied out of concern people would develop an interest in history.

In Pomona, the *zanjas* have been seen by generations of children on field trips to Palomares' two adobes. The adobes are open to the public from 2 to 5 p.m. each Sunday.

The longest *zanja* is at La Casa Primera. Two feet wide and almost two feet deep, it's lined with rock and has a bottom of dirt and pebbles (and dead leaves and weeds).

The *zanja* begins at the corner of Park and McKinley, then winds behind the house. It passes under a fig tree reputed to be 150 years old and disappears into the pavement at the rear of the property.

A *zanja* runs through it.

Hey, that could be a movie!

'Pomona A to Z': letters on the letters

How can there be another column after Z? I wrote an epilogue column – published July 3, 2005 – of reader reaction to the series.

The comment from the Ontario reader cheesed me off – did he think, after I'd devoted a year to writing favorably about Pomona, that I'd find his snobbish put-down of Pomona to be hilarious? – so I relished zinging him back. But everyone else was nice, and Judi Guizado and Ruth Wells' letters are so brilliant I'm thrilled to re-present them.

I say in this column that there will "probably" be more "A to Z" series, but there weren't. It began to seem impractical to delve that deeply into one city over 26 columns. But, I'll never say never, and in light of my remark that another "A to Z" may arrive when you least expect it, maybe it will arrive when I least expect it too.

"Pomona A to Z" taught me a lot about Pomona, and with all I've learned since then, it's only become clearer how little I knew when I wrote it. But I hope you've enjoyed reading, or rereading, these columns anyway.

Readers 'letter rip' on A to Z

With the 26-part series "Pomona A to Z" having ended, some readers are having trouble letting go.

"Don't you have any more letters?" Pomona Councilman George Hunter asked me after Z for *Zanja*. "Could you do some diphthongs?"

Complex vowel sounds aside, I'm sorry to see the series end too. After all, for 26 Sundays I always knew where my next column was coming from. Now what?

"Perhaps you should reprise 'A to Z' for all Inland Valley cities," C.J. Fogel, a former newsroom colleague, wrote to suggest. "Or how about 'A to Z' but using Khmer, the world's largest alphabet? Moving on from '*tha*,' we now have '*pha*'..."

Well, yours truly wrote about pho, so why not *pha*?

I brought my A-game to "A to Z," hoping to have fun – and I did – while nudging people into looking at Pomona in a new light. It was successful, at least up to a point.

Jim Downs, a 28-year resident of Ontario, said he enjoyed reading about the valley's other big city.

"I found out some interesting things about Pomona each week, and I even thought about going to see one or two of them," Downs wrote. "But then I thought, 'It *is* Pomona!'"

You say that like it's a bad thing.

"An underrated city" is how reader David Fleury described Pomona, and he's got it exactly right.

Fleury, who spent 24 years in Pomona, insisted he learned "so much" from my series, which is quite a compliment. He can't have learned more than I did, though.

I knew very little about Pomona going into "A to Z." Even now I know just a smidge – but it's a good smidge.

Thanks to everyone who nominated people, places and things, by the way. True, I could have done the series without you. But it would have stunk.

Will there be another "A to Z"? Probably.

Downs, the Ontario resident quoted above, requested an "Ontario A to Z."

With such a series, "we could discover some little-known or forgotten facts about Ontario with which we could wow and amaze our friends in other humdrum communities not nearly as interesting as our area! Whaddaya think?"

It's a great idea, but I do have one worry.

What if people from Pomona refuse to check out the attractions because, after all, "It *is* Ontario"?

You may recall that I stole the alphabet concept from a fine, funny PBS documentary by Rick Sebak, "Pittsburgh A to Z."

I recently shipped off all 26 columns to Sebak, who was so excited he wrote me, then called me.

Turns out the Bard of Pittsburgh had already quoted me on the back of the DVD version of "A to Z" (available at www.wqed.org), and how cool is that?

Sebak called my series "totally fun to read" and encouraged me to do more. The "A to Z" concept, incidentally, wasn't even his – a Pittsburgh museum official suggested it.

"You can't copyright the letters of the alphabet," Sebak added cheerfully. "As far as I'm concerned, it's a marvelous gimmick. Take it and run."

When readers least expect it, I will.

But first, I'll let two of you run with it. Because two separate e-mails from two separate readers took an alphabetical approach to critiquing my series.

Judi Guizado wrote:

"I found your columns to be amazing, beatific, classy, delightful, edifying, first-rate, groovy, heartfelt, interesting, joyful, kindhearted, laudable, masterful, neat-o, orderly, praiseworthy, quirky, reminiscent, scandalous – oops, sorry, wrong column; that one's for Pomona's self-imposed pay raise – transcendent, unusual, valiant, well-written, Xeroxable, yatterless and zestful."

Guizado would like to thank the members of the Academy, plus Roget's Thesaurus.

And Ruth Wells chimed in with this:

"Allen's Bulletin Columns Did Effectually Furnish Great Highlights, Interesting Jewels, Knowledge Listing Many Nuances of Pomona's Quintessence – Restaurants, Specifics of our ethnic citizens, Tableaus of Today, Unforgettable, Valued Works of the past, X-cellent Yarns, Zealously told."

I'm awe-struck, blushing, content, dumbfounded, etc.

Now let's let the alphabet rest a bit. We've given it a heckuva workout.

www.ingramcontent.com/pod-product-compliance
Lightning Source LLC
Chambersburg PA
CBHW071113160426
43196CB00013B/2553